To: Clarissa
From: Kinetta Graves
Evans-Mom
☺
Enjoy!

Go Get Yours

A Wake Up Call to Today's Generation and Tomorrow's Future

IVAN JAMES

authorHOUSE®

AuthorHouse™
1663 Liberty Drive
Bloomington, IN 47403
www.authorhouse.com
Phone: 1-800-839-8640

© 2011 Ivan James. All rights reserved.

No part of this book may be reproduced, stored in
a retrieval system, or transmitted by any means
without the written permission of the author.

First published by AuthorHouse 7/18/2011

ISBN: 978-1-4567-5156-2 (e)
ISBN: 978-1-4567-5155-5 (sc)

Library of Congress Control Number: 2011904801

Printed in the United States of America

Any people depicted in stock imagery provided by Thinkstock are models,
and such images are being used for illustrative purposes only.
Certain stock imagery © Thinkstock.

This book is printed on acid-free paper.

Because of the dynamic nature of the Internet, any web addresses or
links contained in this book may have changed since publication and
may no longer be valid. The views expressed in this work are solely those
of the author and do not necessarily reflect the views of the publisher,
and the publisher hereby disclaims any responsibility for them.

Table of Contents

FEATURES	vii
DEDICATION	ix
INTRO	xi

CHAPTERS

Parents: They just don't understand or do they?	1
Fools will be Fools	12
Rise above the Haters	22
Drugs	32
Life Is A Race	44
Get Educated	54
Plan = Goals + Steps	67
Believe----Achieve----Succeed-----Reflect	77
Keep Your Focus	91
No Excuses	106
Think First	117
The Way It Should Be	128

STEP YOUR GAME UP	141
REWIND: TAKE NOTES	150
OUTRO	153
ABOUT THE AUTHOR	157

Features

Parents
Quote(s) – Denzel Washington, Adam Sandler, Ice Cube, Jamie Foxx

Fools will be Fools
Quote(s) – Prince, Nas

Rise above the Haters
Quote(s) – Will Smith, Shawn "Jay-Z" Carter

Drugs feat. Tupac Shakur, Tiger Woods, Len Bias, Earl "DMX" Simmons
Quote(s) – Denzel Washington, Chris Rock

Life is a Race
Quote(s) – T.I., Marcus Garvey

Get Educated feat. Ben Carson, Eddy Curry, Antoine Walker

Have a Plan feat. Master P
Quote(s) – Nas, Ice Cube

Believe feat. Eminem, Daymond John, Barack Obama, Usher Raymond, Sean Diddy Combs, Missy Elliott, Kanye West
Quote(s) – BIG, Kanye West, Allen Iverson

Keep your Focus feat. LeBron James, Nick Cannon, Allen Iverson, OutKast
Quote(s) – Rihanna, Usher Raymond, Aaliyah

No Excuses feat. Michael Dell, Isiah Thomas, Tyler Perry, Bob Johnson, Karl Kani, Catherine Hughes
Quote(s) – Martin Lawrence, Benjamin Franklin

The Way it Should Be feat. Min. Benjamin Muhammed

Dedication

The first day I met Brandon Milford; I was a young, competitive person at Woodham High School in Pensacola, FL. I was an athlete, honor student and also involved in many organizations. Yet, I noticed that there was another young man that was in each of my classes and activities. I noticed that not only did he work as hard as I did, but he worked harder. For years, I strived to be better than him. It took me years to realize that because of him I became not only a better student, but also a better person.

I believe anyone who had the pleasure to meet Brandon could feel the kindness in his heart when they spoke to him. He was a person who always looked for the good in others. He never showed or inflicted negativity towards anyone. Brandon just wanted to see happiness throughout everyone he encountered.

Brandon was never the type of person to feel jealous of another person because of his or her accomplishments. If he didn't achieve a goal or task right away, Brandon would only work harder to achieve or overcome that obstacle. He was more than just an athlete, a Christian, a scholar, an activist in his church, school and community. Brandon was one of my closest friends.

The one thing I will never forget about Brandon is that he believed in doing what was right in life, no matter who was around him. He was the kind of person who remained humble about his accomplishments. I remember in basketball practice when we would have to run a mile around the track. Brandon would almost always overlap everyone, which would make everyone else look bad. I would sometimes ask him why did he work so hard?

Today, I realize that the question I should have asked myself was why couldn't I work harder like Brandon?

In classes such as chemistry, we would sometimes work on assignments. I remember how others and myself may have given up on problems that became too hard or strenuous, yet Brandon would never quit. He would just take his time and eventually develop his answers. Brandon had unbelievable patience and persistence. Through Brandon, I have instilled these traits into my own personality, which have helped me to become a better person.

It hurts me to the bottom of my heart that you are no longer here, but I'm glad to know that you're in heaven smiling down on those that loved you. I hope that this book will be an example for others to follow, the way that you were an example for me.

----In loving memory
Brandon C. Milford
1983 - 2004

Intro

This book was written as an inspiration to today's generation and tomorrow's future. Our young people may not realize just how valuable they are in this world. The sooner you realize your value, the sooner you can begin to build upon it.

This book is considered an alarm clock to alert each young mind to recognize just how much potential you are filled with. Once you realize this potential, you have to take action and begin to nurture it. No longer should you continue to hit the snooze button.

The world is filled with so many people that emphasize the wrong things and spread the wrong messages. Our TVs, radios and web pages broadcast so much negativity that it's almost impossible to filter out anything positive. That's why it is up to our young people to begin a new trend. Our future leaders of tomorrow can lay down the foundation for news that's made to lift us up, not tear us down.

Too many young minds are destroyed by the wrong influences that surround them and their environment. We must take a stand and break this cycle. We have to make the brains and spirits of our young people so strong that they can never be demolished or even tarnished. It may not be an easy task, but it has to be done. No longer can we sit back and fall victim to our circumstances.

Throughout our existence, there will always be a war on illiteracy. We can win this war if we choose to challenge ourselves and our minds to succeed. Stop settling and learn to start striving. Our young generation is filled with so many talents and gifts. We need to work together and move forward, rather than generate conflict amongst each other.

Disputes among our young people should be handled with our minds, not with our fists. We must fight with our brains, not with our hands. An intelligent mind is more powerful than one could ever imagine. A brain can be our biggest muscle and most intimidating force once we put it to use.

This book was not intended to start any type of physical revolt by those who are considered as minorities. Readers should be inspired by the message that is delivered and become encouraged to make a revolution within themselves. Stop accepting the bad hand that life may have dealt you. Get up and strive for what you want within this world.

Each and every day we must strive to exercise our minds to think outside the box. When it comes to our potential, young people should be aware that there are no boundaries. The passion to pursue excellence lies within you. We just have to discover it underneath the layers of pessimism that society pounded on us.

The overall goal from this book is to motivate every reader to think about what lies ahead in the future and plan for success. We may not have what we want today, but we can still achieve great things as we work towards our future. We cannot let our present ruin what awaits us in the next phase of our lives. All it takes is faith, focus and preparation.

Each chapter is filled with potent messages that can be utilized in our daily quest to excel. The information provided within each passage should be considered as inspiration to those in search of it or a wake up call for those in need of it. Every paragraph should be deemed as a written form of motivation to the reader who may just need that extra push. Each sentence is designed to help expand the drive that is already built inside of you.

One should not feel rushed to rapidly read through the pages of this book. Take your time and make sure that you comprehend all of the enclosed content. If you come across a term that you do not understand, please do not just skip over it. Grab a dictionary and read the definition so that you understand the meaning of the word used within the sentence.

This world provides so many avenues that lead to success. All you have to do is find the right avenue and make the effort to stay on it. There's too much opportunity out there for any of us to slip through the cracks. We cannot let negative minds pull us down as long as we keep our minds positioned to climb to the top. We were blessed with all the right equipment. Now it's time for us to use it to our advantage.

No longer can we sit back and keep getting stuck in last place. The time has come in your life to catch up and demand to take the lead.

Parents: They just don't understand or do they?

We would go places. And I would wild out. And she would say, "Act like you've been somewhere." And then when I would act the fool, she would beat me. She would whup me. And she could get an Oscar for the way she whupped me because she was great at it. And after she whipped me, she would talk to me and tell me why she whipped me. She said I want you to be a southern gentleman. She still talks to me now. Only now, she talks to me, in my dreams. And I can't wait to go to sleep tonight because we got a lot to talk about. I love you.

-------Jamie Foxx

[2005 Academy Awards acceptance speech for Best Actor in a Leading Role]

It is Monday morning and your mama is yelling for you to get up to go to school. You hate going to school, but mama won't hear it. You probably ask yourself, why won't mama just leave me alone? Don't worry, that's a normal situation.

Everyone hates doing something. Most kids just happen to hate school. Parents know that. When they were your age, they hated school too. Yet, your parents know that people that have an education have more advantages than people without one. That's why it's so important to your parents that you get an education.

Everyday parents go to work and compete with people that may be more educated than them. Your parents want to provide for you the best way possible. They know that an education gives them that opportunity. That's why they want you to get the best education and grades so that you'll be able to provide for yourself one day.

By Any Means Necessary

The funniest and most embarrassing thing a parent can do to a child is to come up to their school to discipline them. Have you ever seen when someone's mama or daddy came into your class because their child was acting a fool? Talk about angry, those parents look like their ready to hurt everybody.

The funniest thing is trying to figure out whose mama it is. You could always figure it out because it's usually the kid that's looking like he's doing some work. One time, a boy's mama came in class to see how her son was doing. When she found out that he was disrupting class, she grabbed him by the arm and took this thick belt out of her purse.

Then she took him to the bathroom, which was in the classroom and tore his butt up! All the kids in the class were laughing for the rest of the day. Here's how it went down.

Mama: How's Gary doing in class?

Ms. Peters: Well, Gary seems to have trouble concentrating in class. He disrupts the class quite often.

Mama: He's disrupting class! Let's see if we can fix this problem. Gary front and center!

Parents: They just don't understand or do they?

As Gary walks toward his mama she takes out a large black belt.

Mama: Boy didn't I tell you about your mouth!

She grabs him and takes him into the bathroom. She whips out the belt.

Mama: Whap!

Gary: Aah!

The class is dying with laughter.

No matter how old you get, you can never forget a moment like this. Gary never disrupted the class again.

People think it seems embarrassing, but parents sometimes have to go the extra mile to keep you on the right track. A lot of kids don't have parents that will take the time to discipline them. Some parents don't think it's necessary and some parents just don't care.

It is important that you understand why parents discipline you. The reason is because they don't want to see you end up like the fools that they see. They want to see you be successful. So they help you stay focused, BY ANY MEANS NECESSARY.

Sometimes we sleep on the importance of school. Since we're young, we may not recognize the value of a solid education. Parents see it differently, just as we do later on in life.

An education is like a key. It can open the door to many opportunities. Not only just opportunities, but an education encourages others to show you respect. You want to know why? An education takes *commitment, dedication* and *will-power*. Believe it or not, but not everyone has these qualities.

A lot of people quit school because they do not have the heart to stick with it. When classes get too hard or teachers get too tough, they drop out. That's why you see parents get so emotional when their kids graduate. They're proud that you fought through the rough times and didn't give in to the pressure.

Your parents respect what you had to go through to earn that diploma. Not only do your parents respect what you've done, but others do as well. Family, friends, church members, even your peers recognize the significant mountain you climbed.

Last but not least, you should respect and take pride in reaching the important milestone of graduating. And when you do reach it, make sure that you *recognize* and *thank your parents* for helping you to earn and value the importance of an education.

Been there, Done that

Your parents only tell you to do what is right because they have been through what you are going through. They want to help you avoid the problems that they've already dealt with in life. The number one goal for your parents is for you to be a success.

Parents want to make sure that you achieve more in life than they have. To them, you're their greatest gift to the world. It's important that the whole world knows how special you are to their life and everyone else. In short, you are the future of the family.

You might not believe it, but everything you have gone through in life or will go through, chances are your parents have been through it. A lot of times we feel like our parents didn't deal with sex. How else do you think you got here?

Issues like sex, drugs, peer pressure and rebellion are

Parents: They just don't understand or do they?

stuff that your parents dealt with when they were in your shoes. Not only that, but some parents had it a lot worse than you could imagine. Do you ever hear people say that they had a rough life and they want to make sure that their kids have a better life than they did? Believe it or not, but parents mean it!

Some of the opportunities that we have in life today did not even exist when your parents were coming up. Today, we have better technology and resources than they could've ever imagined. That's why parents don't allow kids to come up with excuses because they know it's just what it is, *an excuse*. Think about it.

When your parents were in school they did not have the resources that we use everyday today. For example, when your teacher assigns you a research project, what's the first thing you do? Like most of us, when we have to research anything we run straight to the computer and look it up on the internet. And you know exactly what comes next, *COPY* and *PASTE*!

In your parent's days, there was NO *internet*. They had to search for what they wanted to know the hard way, by book. Parents had to read and search through the fine print of numerous books just to find what we can find now in 10 seconds. No wonder parents don't want to cut us slack.

We get more than enough slack from technology. But some of us still have a problem with taking the time to search on the web. As young adults, we have to take advantage of our resources. We got to get our MIND RIGHT.

We have so many more resources available to us that our parents never had when they were coming up in the world. From the Internet, cell phones, iPods, etc. The world is literally at our fingertips. We find out whatever we want in a matter of minutes. This generation should utilize the resources provided by our parents' generation.

Our young people should use these resources and accept the responsibility of adding on to it.

Each generation is responsible for improving the way of life for the next generation. Your grandparents improved our methods of transportation. Your parents improved our methods of communication. What will the young people of your generation bring to the table? The opportunities for improvement are unlimited. We must take what our parents left behind and make an effort to go above and beyond their achievements.

Sometimes your parents may not agree with what you want to do. Help them understand what you like to do and why you like to do it. Ask them why they don't agree with what you do. If they see the benefits of what you do and that it makes you happy, they may support you in it.

Give them a chance to help you understand their opinion. In return, they'll be willing to listen to your views. Try and respect the choices your parents make. Believe it or not, the majority of the decisions made by your parents are in your best interest.

Learning Responsibility

Parents want to help you become a good person. They tell you to rake the leaves, clean the bathroom and wash the dishes because they want you to learn responsibility. They know how important it is for you to be responsible.

Do you know one of the biggest differences between a fool and a leader? Fools aren't responsible. Some fools have parents that try to teach them responsibility and a lot of fools don't. In the long run you'll see how young fools end up because of one missing ingredient, *responsibility*.

Responsibility leads to another argument that we have as young people. One of our biggest issues as young people is the way that we feel we are treated. As young adults, we want others to treat us like adults. Here's a simple rule to follow. If you want to be treated like an adult you have to show it. One way that you can show it is by being responsible.

Do your best to become more responsible. If you know that you're supposed to be home at a certain time, honor that responsibility. If you're supposed to cut the grass every Saturday, honor that responsibility. If you have to look after your younger brother or sister after school, honor that responsibility. Get into the habit of doing things without having to be asked to do them. This is called *initiative*.

One excuse that parents should never use is that someone else's influence made us commit trouble. This means that parents cannot blame others for the actions of their kids. A lot of parents try to blame society for the mistakes made by their kids. That's wrong!

Some parents not only blame society, but they even attempt to blame music for trouble created by their kids. Think about how silly that sounds. How can you blame someone else's music for teaching a kid to do wrong?

Parents need to focus on teaching kids what's right instead of blaming music for teaching what's wrong. Nothing should have more influence on a kid than their parents, especially not music. A song or a music video doesn't last longer than three or four minutes. So how can you put the blame on music? It just doesn't make sense.

Parents should not allow kids to become influenced from what is aired on the radio or played on TV. Our parents cannot allow our TVs and radios to raise us, nor can we allow it as young people. Any parent that blames movies, music or videos for influencing their child to do wrong should first accept the blame for allowing something or someone else to become a parent to their child.

If I'm more of an influence to your son as a rapper than you are as a father…you got to look at yourself as a parent.

------Ice Cube

It is the responsibility of parents to establish morals and discipline within the household. No matter what is said on the radio or on TV, parents are expected to identify the values and standards that one should live by to reach excellence. Even if the most negative song is in heavy radio rotation, a listener who has values should understand that what he or she is listening to is nothing more than a song. Lyrics within a song should never influence anyone to do wrong.

To honor our parents can be even more difficult when we see them setting bad examples or doing what is considered as wrong. Certain parents are victims of drugs, alcohol, gambling, etc. These parents abuse themselves and may eventually even abuse their children. This is considered as wrong as wrong can be. Under these circumstances, there is no perfect response or suggestions that can be given. A person should not have to honor parents that cannot even honor themselves. Anyone who is in this type of situation should be encouraged only to do what's right.

A parent could enforce morals and values just by being an example for their child to follow. In all honesty, it is not right for a parent to tell a child how wrong it is to smoke when they themselves are firing up two packs of cigarettes every day. Something is just not right when a man tells his son to leave alcohol alone, but every night he himself is draining a six-pack of beer down his throat.

How silly is it for a parent to tell their child not to use profanity if the parent is cursing every night when talking on their cell phone? Young people must ultimately choose to do right. Yet, the choice would be so easy if parents choose to do right themselves.

Parents should instill in our young people to have a mind for themselves. No way can someone be influenced to do wrong if they've been taught the right values. Encourage your parents to give you the proper guidance so that you'll be prepared to make the best possible decisions in this world.

Single Parent ~ Double Duty

As we move further into the 21st century, the trend of being raised in single parent households will only rise higher and higher. People are out having sex and bringing babies into the world without any intention of getting married. For the record, it is unfair for kids to have to be raised this way.

Kids should have the right to be raised in one household with both parents. It's unfair when one parent has to play two roles in the life of their child. Kids being raised in single-parent homes are receiving the first of the world's many lessons. The first and most important lesson is that life is not fair.

The level of success or status of our parents should not determine the success that our young people can achieve. Kids who come from the worst conditions still have the ability to shine. Whether inside or outside of the classroom, a student's potential cannot be diminished no matter how bad a parent's circumstances might be. Some of the most successful people in the world came from nothing. Yet, they were able to make something out of nothing.

I never had a speech from my father 'this is what you must do or shouldn't do' but I just learned to be led by example. My father wasn't perfect.

--- Adam Sandler

Parents are Human, not Perfect

Regardless of how we see our parents, we must always remember that our parents are not perfect. Our parents make mistakes. They have good days and bad days. Parents never expect their kids to be perfect so young people should never expect for parents to be perfect. Give them a chance the same way parents never stop taking chances on you.

The most corrupt people in this world have parents who will still stand behind them. Some people may disagree with someone sticking by a bad person, but the role of a parent is to always support and protect their children. As young people, we must always support and honor our parents. The Bible even reads that we must honor our mother and father so that our days may be longer. No matter what opinion you might have, you cannot argue with what God has already asked of you.

Show your parents that you appreciate what they do for you. The words "thank you" are two of the most powerful words in the world when put together. Use them when someone deserves to hear it from you. Your parents brought you into this world through love. Every great thing you hope to achieve in life would not be possible had your parents never created you. Wouldn't you agree that this deserves a thank you?

Good Parents:
1. Keep you in check
2. Teach you responsibility
3. Support the goals that you set for yourself
4. Teach you not to be a quitter
5. Help you understand your priorities
6. Make you maximize your potential

****

Parents: They just don't understand or do they?

Take Notes:

Your parents only tell you to do what's right because they have been through what you are going through. They want to help you avoid the problems that they've already dealt with in life.

What are some common disagreements that you have with your parents?
Would you say that you need to communicate more with your parents?

Are your parents supportive of you when you set forth to achieve your goals?

My mother never gave up on me. I messed up in school so much they were sending me home, but my mother sent me right back.

--- Denzel Washington

Fools will be Fools

Nobody says you have to be ganstas and hoes. Read more, learn more, change the globe.

------Nas

Have you ever met someone that always talks about what they could have done if they really wanted to? You know they never attempted to achieve what they say they can, but they claim it would be easy for them to do. That person is called a **fool**. They never attempt to try something. Instead of completing an achievement or goal, they act like they could've done it if they WANTED to. Don't be a fool.

A **fool** is someone that always claims that he or she is too real. They tell a person like it is and claim that they don't hold back for anyone. Believe me when I say, that person is a FOOL.

People that are too real end up in one of three places: dead, jail, or living with their mama. Fools don't have any priorities or goals. They just live from day to day. They can't keep a job because they can't come on time or do what they are asked to do without complaining. They'll be the people that you see that come to school looking like they just woke up. Hair not brushed or combed, wrinkled clothes and sagging pants are usually the standard appearance of a fool.

Fools do not believe in book bags, so they come to

Fools will be Fools

school with ONE folder. How can you have five classes in one day and bring ONE folder? Have you ever dressed out for P.E. and saw a group of guys that show up in their same school clothes when its time to participate? Instead of changing clothes like the coach says, they come to P.E. without a change of clothes and take an "F" for the day. That's a fool!

Regardless of what they are asked to do, fools have a problem doing it. They have to be the one that's difficult at all times. Take this time to reflect on the people around you. Can you think of any fools? Have you ever been considered a fool?

A fool usually always seems to find something wrong with everything. Fools love to complain about a birthday, gift, dinner or anything that gives them the opportunity to complain.

Fools should not be hard to identify in a large group of people because they love to talk loud, or as they call it "loud talking." Fools "loud talk" because they don't know how to keep quiet in situations where they should be. While other students are in class to learn, a fool comes to class to make noise and disrupt everyone. In school, the goal of a fool is to make everyone become just as ignorant as they are. Rather than attempt to learn, a fool automatically complains, "I don't wanna' learn this mess!"

Teacher: Class, today we're going to read about….

Fool: Why we got to read again? Didn't we already read yesterday?

See what I mean? A fool will complain even before there is anything to complain about. The worst fact about fools is that a young fool will eventually grow up to become an old fool.

When they get older, fools still complain about everything. Usually when a fool gets a job, he ends up losing it. It's hard for fools to keep jobs because a job requires them to follow rules. Unfortunately, rules and fools just don't seem to be a good match.

Boss: Derek, you've been late almost everyday this week. This type of behavior cannot continue!

Fool: Aw, come on. I got here right after you. If I've been late, then you've been late too.

See this is an example of a fool at his most ignorant stage. A fool can't follow rules and a fool doesn't know when to be quiet. Young fools are guaranteed to become old fools. Old fools usually end up living with their mom for 20 – 30 years, while everyone else goes out and accomplishes their goals. Think about this picture, a grown man living in the basement of his mother's house.

Mom: CJ, clean up this room! After you clean that room, get in the kitchen and wash the dishes! Then, take out the trash.

Fool: Mama I'ma do it. Let me finish watching TV.

It's pretty obvious that something is wrong with this picture. You have a grown man living at home with his mama. If he had a job, he probably wouldn't be asked to do chores. Instead, he's wasting his time watching TV, like a fool. Remember that TV wasn't made for you to watch all day and waste time. Believe it or not, but TV can become a bad influence.

Young people need to realize that the shows that they

watch on TV play a part in their behavior. On TV you have shows, even cartoons that have characters cursing and using words such as *n*gga*. African-Americans have spent hundreds of years trying to stop people from using this word. Now you have the word being used in cartoons for kids to hear. That's not cool. It's ignorant.

Cartoons and shows today are preaching ignorance to young minorities. In the 1990s you had shows like *Fresh Prince, Martin, Living Single, Family Matters, Parent Hood, Moesha* and more. What made these shows popular was their ability to reflect the different lifestyles of single African-Americans and families. These shows were special because they were humorous, not degrading. Today you have cartoons that give a negative impression to society and even worse, our own culture.

Being a fool can only take you so far in life. For example, have you ever seen somebody holding up a sign that says *work for food?* Well, when you see someone holding up that sign, take a good look at that person. Believe it or not, but that person used to be a young kid who couldn't stop acting a fool in class. What's even sadder is that they grew up to be old fools. Think about it.

Why would someone hold up a sign that says *work for food?* What do you think parents and other people in America work for? They sure aren't working because they enjoy it. They're working to provide food for themselves and their family. So why should a homeless person think any differently? That's foolish! If they can't get a job and work for food, why should someone believe that they'll "work for food?"

Most of the problems that fools have are brought on from the decisions they make. Here's another example of a fool in action.

Tom: Aye Joe, why you ain't playing on the team no more?

Fool: Man that coach is crazy! He can't coach.

Tom: So that's why you quit?

Fool: Nah, he kicked me off the team because I wouldn't run laps like everyone else.

This is an example of how a fool shows his silly behavior. Rather than participate with his teammates, a fool has to rebel and show ignorance.

Fools Waste Time

Fools usually spend their days hanging outside all day doing exactly what they want to do, nothing. Why do people like to chill outside on the porch all day? How often have you seen a bunch of fools sitting outside smoking and drinking? It's as if people don't have anything more important to do. It doesn't make sense for someone to just hang out all the time.

In our society today, we need to understand exactly what we are doing and why we do it. Are we hanging out on the steps because we haven't seen our friends in a while and we want to spend time with them? If not, it's probably because of the number one reason; we think that we don't have anything better to do.

Young people should be encouraged to use their time wisely. Time is a precious resource that you can never recover. No matter how much money you have, you can never buy back time.

Fools Mismanage $$$

Speaking of money, fools can make the worst decisions when it comes to spending it. No matter how much something can cost, a fool will still pay money for it. This mistake is one that we all must break. Young America, we have to wake up and think about the choices that we make.

Corporate America views our culture as a *cash cow*. They make billions of dollars off our culture each year. The reason why is because of our buying decisions. They influence us to buy things that we don't need. They know that we don't need what they sell us, but they know that we'll buy it anyway. Think about it. How many of your friends spend their good money on *Air Jordan's* each year? You probably couldn't even keep count.

It is embarrassing how terrible our decisions are when it comes to money. It's as if we don't think. When you look at the clothes that you purchase, learn to also look at the country that they were manufactured in. If it says Korea, Indonesia, China, or any other foreign country, you should know that you are paying way too much for that product.

Foreign countries have the lowest minimum wages in the world. The term *"sweat shop"* was created from the minimum wage that people make working overseas. But when it comes to buying products, what's made overseas can cost almost 10 times as much in the USA. For example, a shirt that cost $3 in Indonesia can cost $30 in the U.S.

This should make you think more about how corporate America is robbing you. They're making a 200% profit off of you when you decide to buy their high priced clothing. Think about what you could do with the extra money that you gave them. Understand that it's not worth it.

You see people walking around in designer fashions that

cost hundreds of dollars, but what you don't see is them missing payments on their bills for the month. They may look fly when you see them, but chances are they don't have much to show for themselves.

Chris: Aye cuz, you seen dem new *Js* (Air Jordans) that came out?

Larry: Yeah, they clean. They already sold out at the mall.

Prince: I'm glad I reserved my pair. My *Js* are in the box waiting for me. They fresh.

Chris: How much you paid?

Prince: Fool, you know how much they cost. I paid bout *$200.00*. But they clean though! They gon be hating when I wear em to school tomorrow.

This is an example of how we misuse our money. We spend money on things that we DON'T NEED. Think about it. $200.00 for a pair of sneakers! You could buy at least *three pairs* of shoes for that price.

Wise people on the other hand play it smart. They set a budget for how much they plan to spend before they even go shopping. They're budget is a plan; and they stick to it! They understand that the purpose of shopping is to buy what they need and they know that they don't NEED to overspend their hard-earned money. We don't understand this concept until we get older. But some of us that get older still don't get it.

(Twenty years later)

Fools will be Fools

Prince: What up boy, I just got paid! Let's go to Biloxi and hit the casino.

Larry: Prince, don't you have to pay off your credit card debt. Plus, what about your rent? You said they were sending you eviction notices.

Prince: Man, don't worry about all that. Let's go have some fun and spend this money. After all, you only live once.

It's important that you don't trap yourself into a foolish way of thinking. The reason is because once you start to think like a fool, you'll begin to act like a fool. That's how simple it is! I encourage you to surround yourself with positive and balanced people. A balanced person is someone that is intelligent, but still "hip" to what's going on in society.

A balanced person knows how to make friends, but is aware of the people that they need to stay away from. These types of people are good for friendship and also connections. If they know about what you want to do in life, they can find a way to help you or even provide you with an opportunity.

A fool cannot provide you with anything but downfall and ignorance. So do your best to surround yourself with people who are balanced. They can open more doors for you than you can ever imagine.

In order to achieve excellence, you cannot portray a fool. If you have friends that are fools, be careful! Make sure that they don't pull you into their foolish ways. You want to keep a good head on your shoulders. There's nothing corny about that.

Through school and through life, you will meet people that will tell you what's cool and what's not cool. Place yourself around people that are looking to achieve excellence. That's cool. People that don't want to do what's right in life are losers.

Winner vs. Fool

(Difference between a winner and a fool)

Winner

1. A winner makes sacrifices to win the goal.
2. A winner keeps their focus on the main objective.
3. A winner dedicates their time to accomplishing their mission.
4. A winner does everything possible in the attempt to achieve their goal.
5. A winner works well with others.

Fool

1. A fool won't sacrifice.
2. A fool is unable to focus because his mind is cluttered with foolishness.
3. A fool can't dedicate his time to anything.
4. If a fool can't achieve it on the first attempt, he assumes it's not possible to achieve.
5. A fool lets "others" work well, so that he doesn't have to work at all.

• •

Take Notes:

You cannot achieve greatness if you spend all your time hanging out with losers. Don't allow yourself to waste time.

Fools will be Fools

Let fools "do what they do." Just remember that if you want to succeed you must "do you."

Final Thought:

A fool is born based on his or her actions and choices. When you choose to do wrong versus right, you are giving birth to the fool in you. When your actions begin to destroy your future, you are raising the fool in you. The people that surround you can be the most devilish and foolish people around. Yet, you are the one that controls your actions and choices. You can never stop making the decision to stand on your own feet and do what's right. You were born with your own brain. Why not put it to use?

Cool means being able to hang with yourself. All you have to ask yourself is 'Is there anybody I'm afraid of? Is there anybody who if I walked into a room and saw, I'd get nervous?' If not, then you're cool.

--- Prince

Rise above the Haters

Jealousy's a weak emotion. When the grass is cut, the snakes will show.

----- Jay-Z

Have you ever watched the movie Boyz in the Hood? Do you remember the beginning of the movie? In the beginning, the young Trey Styles is in class. While in class, Trey is showing off his foolish arrogance. The teacher soon asks if he would like to teach, since he can't stop making comments. Rather than turn down the challenge, the young Trey accepts the opportunity to teach his peers.

As Trey walks to the front of the classroom, his friend shows his jealousy and hatred. When Trey begins to do a good job teaching the class about Africa, his friend begins to interrupt and make jokes. Rather than support his friend for his intelligence, the hater has to try to disrupt and discourage him.

Teacher: Trey, would you like to come up and teach the class?

Trey: Yeah, I can do that.
(As Trey walks to the front of the class, his friend develops an angry look on his face.)

Teacher: Very well, come on up. Instruct us.

(Trey takes a long pointer and points to Africa on a large overhead map in front of the class.)

Trey: Does anyone know what the name of this place is?

(A young girl raises her hand.)

Young girl: That's Africa.

Trey: That's right that's Africa. But did you know that Africa was the place where the first body was found? That means everyone is originally from Africa. Everybody. All y'all.

Hater: I ain't from Africa, I'm from Crenshaw Mafia.

(The class begins to laugh.)

Trey: Like it or not, you're from Africa.

Hater: I ain't from Africa, you from Africa you African booty scratcher!

See how jealous his friend became of Trey's ability to shine before the class. This scenario should provide you with a clear example of what a hater is.

Definition of a Hater

Why is it whenever you come up with an idea or begin to think outside the box, others try to discourage you? It's almost as if the people that you know don't want to see you doing any better than them. Notice the expressions of people around you when you're acknowledged for your achievements in school, sports or things that you excel in.

Not everyone will hope that you achieve excellence. Those people are called **haters**.

Haters hate to see other people receive recognition when they themselves are not included. The term "haters" is an acronym for those having anger towards everyone reaching success. Regardless of how good of a person you are, people will hate on you. It's hard for haters to see others do well in life. They hate it! That's why they're called haters.

Types of Haters

Haters are the types of people that should inspire you. There are two types of haters: *loud haters* and *rat haters*. A *loud* hater will let any and everyone know that he or she hates on someone. If you're at a game, he's the one yelling, "Anybody could've made that!" Whenever he sees a girl he couldn't have, he yells out "she ain't cute!"

A *rat* hater is a hater that "hates" quietly, instead of letting the person they hate know about it. They only talk about someone whenever that person isn't around to hear it. They spread rumors and lies about people. In other words, a rat hater is a coward. Rat haters are afraid to tell someone that they have a problem with them.

Rat haters have no confidence and usually fail in the long run at whatever they attempt. They'll be the ones that you'll see in the future with no family, no children and working in the same company with few promotions. Can you think of any haters that you know? Have you ever been a hater?

Here is an example of a hater in the act of hating:

(In a 7th grade classroom, Eric is recognized in class for an "A" that he received on his test.)

Rise above the Haters

Teacher: Congratulations Eric. You received the only "A" in the class!

Eric: Thanks Ms. Jones.

Sheila: Nice job Eric. I think I need to start studying with you!

Loud Hater: Man, he probably cheated! I got a C and I didn't even study.

It is obvious how the loud hater didn't hesitate to let everyone know how he felt. Now let's look at this scene with a rat hater.

Teacher: Congratulations Eric. You received the only "A" in the class!

Eric: Thanks Ms. Jones.

Blake: Man I wish I had studied harder.

Rat Hater (whispers): Hey Blake…. I saw Eric looking in his pockets during the test. He probably cheated.

Let's look at this scene with a fool. See what changes take place.
(The teacher then passes out the rest of the graded test papers. She spots Tim's paper, *the fool,* and frowns as she folds it up and hands it to him. She tries not to embarrass him of his "F.")

Blake: Aye Tim, what did you get?

Tim: Man, I don't care nothing bout that test. Forget this class. Forget school. After school, I'ma holla at Sheila. You saw how she was looking at me?

You have to watch these haters out here. Haters do not want to educate themselves, but they'll get angry at others for wanting to learn. When someone offers them help, they sometimes don't appreciate it. Check out this next example.

> **Teacher**: Steve, could you help Dominic finish his reading assignment.
> *(The boys walk over to the reading table in the back of the classroom.)*
>
> **Steve**: Okay, which part of the assignment are you having trouble with?
>
> **Hater**: Man what! What makes you think I need help? You think you're so smart. Go take your smart ass and help yourself!

One of the biggest characteristics of a hater is instigating. Why is it whenever an argument breaks out others have to start encouraging those two people to fight, instead of resolving the issue? Have you ever watched two people argue and then see another person come over and try to push them into fighting? Rather than watch someone fight another, try to prevent the fight from even starting.

Here's an example, Ben and Deshawn are arguing over the basketball game they lost in P.E.

> **Ben**: Man, learn how to pass the ball! You know you can't shoot!

Deshawn: Don't worry bout my shooting! If it wasn't for your defense, we would've won!

Jay (*hater*): Ben, how you gon' let this dude clown you like that. Man show him what time it is!

See what I mean. Rather than try to help his peers resolve their issue; Jay has to start trouble. Haters love to start fights and make others start fights. It takes a lot of strength and courage for a person to walk away from a confrontation, something that haters don't have. Walking away doesn't make you a punk, instead it shows that you have discipline.

When you walk away from a fight, you show others that you are in control of yourself and your actions. People that succumb to fighting prove that they don't have full control of themselves. Falling into the trap of fighting shows that a person is weak minded. Think about it. If fighting is the *only* way that you know how to solve problems, then it shows that you aren't strong enough to deal with your situations intelligently.

As you get older, you will realize that people who only know how to fight end up in two places, *dead* or in *jail*. If fighting is the only way to solve your problem, at least make sure that the pros outweigh the cons. In other words, make sure that you stand to gain more from the outcome than you will lose. People may not realize it, but there are ways that you can avoid a fight and not look like a punk. You just have to be smart about the situation and outsmart your foes, or enemies. Here's an example below.

Craig: What's up fool! I ain't bout that talking! You gon have to show me some hands!

Terrance: Man ain't nobody thinking bout you man. You handle yo business and I'll handle mine.

Notice in this example how Terrance did not run from the situation. He took time to address it and then de-fuse it. He didn't let Craig pressure him into fighting or other punishment. He let Craig know that he had his priorities in check and that Craig wasn't one of them.

In life you don't have to be a coward to turn down a challenge. Just face the situation and handle it accordingly. But if you run away from your situations, then you are portraying a COWARD. Do not get it wrong.

Running away from your problems is a coward move! A coward deserves no respect whatsoever. It's funny how in the movies they show white kids getting punked by other white kids. The bigger kids force the smaller kids to give up their lunch money. If you see any of this behavior portrayed in a movie, GET UP and LEAVE or TURN OFF THE MOVIE.

Never ever pay someone to leave you alone. Not only are you giving up your money, you're giving up your dignity. And believe it or not, once you become a coward it'll become harder for you to change. It'll become even harder for you to gain back your dignity. Even when you get older, people will still push over you. To prevent that from ever happening, stick to the rules listed below.

Rules of the game:

- Never run from anyone.
- Never pay someone not to mess with you.
- Face your situations and handle them, rather than run from them.

One thing you definitely cannot do is let a hater take you out of your game. The best way to handle a hater is to let him take his self out. Believe it or not, but most haters are jealous because they envy you. A hater tries to shine when they're around people they think are their friends.

Then when they feel confident, they try to get some attention. As the late entertainer Bernie Mac would say, that's "*false confidence.*" When they see somebody else shining, they try to gain attention by putting that person down. In other words, they have to put other people down to build themselves up.

Anyone should be able to recognize that if you have to put others down to make yourself look good, you're not just a hater, you're also a LAME.

Stand-up guy vs. Hater

Stand-up guy

1. A stand-up guy not only achieves, but he also helps others achieve.
2. A stand-up guy's goal is to bring "up" the hopes of his peers.
3. A stand-up guy gets attention because of his positive manner.
4. A stand-up guy becomes acquainted with other people and networks with them.
5. The ultimate goal for a stand-up guy is to stand on top while helping others stand with him.

Hater

1. A hater hates to see someone achieve the things in life that he never could.
2. A hater's goal is to bring down the hopes of others.

3. A hater wants attention, but does not know how to get it in a positive manner.
4. Haters make assumptions about others, rather than attempt to learn and become acquainted with other people.
5. The ultimate goal for a hater is to make everyone else think exactly the way that he does.

Here is an activity that may help you identify how supportive your friends are and whether or not they may be haters. Make a list of your friends and a table with three columns. Label the three columns *positive, negative* and *don't know*. Place your friends in the following columns based on their attitudes and how they act around you.

Positive	Negative	Don't Know
Jason	Keyshawn	EJ
Sam	BJ	Tony
Terry	Jerry	Dwayne

After completing this activity, you should have a clear understanding of who will really have your back. Remember that you can achieve any goal that you want to. What will motivate you is learning from and being around positive people. You can't learn anything positive from a negative person. Negative people will only give you a negative outlook on your goals and your dreams.

One of the best solutions for removing from negativity is to focus on you. See what improvements you can make within yourself and build upon it. If someone else has achieved what you want, allow that to inspire you to work harder instead of letting it anger you. If there is someone who makes good grades and gets a lot of attention from

Rise above the Haters

the ladies, respect it rather than find reasons to hate on it. Look at ways you can step your game up before you take shots at someone else. Find better use for your time instead of looking to criticize.

In order to be successful you cannot be a hater. Hating on someone else's achievements will only prevent you from achieving any success of your own. If you spend your time worrying about someone else, you won't have time to accomplish your dreams. Instead of hating someone for what they're achieving, take time to get to know that person. They may be able to help you with your goals.

The ultimate step that you can make to prevent hating is to get acquainted with the person you see shining. You might be able to see how that person achieved what it is that you want. You can *never* know too many people. However, if you're around haters or in a hating environment, GET AWAY. Separate yourself from that crowd. Begin looking for new people to hang with. It'll feel strange for a little while, but it's worth it in the long run.

****

Take Notes:

You may be able to murder a hater, but you can't murder hate. Arm yourself with knowledge, education and enlightenment. That's the best way to deal with a hater.

Throughout life people will make you mad, disrespect you and treat you bad. Let God deal with the things they do, cause hate in your heart will consume you too.

------Will Smith

Drugs

I don't get high, but sometimes I wish I did. That way, when I messed up in life I would have an excuse. But right now there's no rehab for stupidity.

------Chris Rock

Nobody likes to hear that drugs are not cool. You want to be cool, just like your friends want to be cool. That's normal. You can be cool without being involved with drugs. But let's breakdown what a drug is.

A **drug** is anything that has control over your actions and behavior. When you can no longer think clearly or are aware of your actions, you are on drugs. A drug can be more than just alcohol or crack cocaine; it can be a bad relationship, violent music, or a bad temper. All of these things are normal, but what's important is to make sure that they don't affect your judgment.

Sex is a Drug

Believe it or not, but sex and pornography can even be considered as forms of drugs. It's so easy for our minds to develop a craving for sex or viewing sexual activity. The right (or wrong) thought can send all of the blood from our head straight down to what hangs between our legs. I'm not

Drugs

saying that thinking about sex is abnormal. Young people should be expected to have sexual desires.

Sex becomes a drug when we focus on it too much. The more that sex dominates our mind, the more powerful of a drug it can become. When magazines, television and the internet become restaurants for your appetite for porn, then there is a problem. When you spend all of your time plotting on who you're going to have sex with, then there is a problem.

The late Tupac Shakur's biggest drug was an addiction to women. Before reaching the peak of his career, women were literally throwing themselves at a 22-year old Tupac. The temptation of sex is a tough challenge for any man, but even tougher when it is constantly offered to you.

Even boxing greats Mike Tyson and Evander Holyfield fell victim to sex addiction as Tupac Shakur did. His addiction was costly when he was charged with sexual abuse in 1993. Had he not served time for this charge and needed bail from Suge Knight's Deathrow Records, many believe he might still be with us today.

Sex can become just as addictive and life changing as any pill or powder you can find. Just ask golf legend Tiger Woods. Woods will probably go down as one of the richest athletes ever. Throughout his career he has earned a fortune.

Yet, with all the millions earned Tiger paid a heavy cost when exposed for his addiction to sex. His craving for sex with other women ultimately cost him his marriage and family. In 2010, Tiger's wife filed for divorce and walked away with half of the fortune earned by the pro golfer.

You see the bad thing about drugs is not just the fact that you are using them. What makes it bad is the control that they have over you. People that use crack or cocaine lose the ability to think clearly. They can only think about how and where are they going to get more crack or cocaine.

Weed becomes just as controlling. People think that weed isn't powerful, but it is. When you start spending money on weed when it should be spent on your needs, then there's a problem! The problem is that you're spending your good *green* on bad *green*.

As hard as it is for us to stay focused on our goals, drugs will only make it more difficult. Drugs will throw off your focus and soon throw off your dreams. Even though it sounds corny, drugs are not your friends.

Friends or Foes

One thing you definitely need to understand is that people that tempt you to do drugs are not your friends. No matter how many drugs they use, a friend would still care enough about you not to encourage you to use them. A friend would even make sure that you don't use drugs because they know the negative effect they have. Most people that use drugs have a negative effect on others.

Believe it or not, the people that persuade you to do drugs are haters. Think about it. If a person is doing drugs, they've either become failures or soon will be. They see that you have goals and dreams, something they no longer have. What would make them feel even better would be to see you fail like them. Since they're destroying their life, they assume they might as well help you destroy yours. So remember this the next time someone offers you to "*hit that.*"

Leonard "Len" Bias will probably go down as one of the greatest basketball players to never play an NBA game. Many compared him to the great Michael Jordan long before Kobe

Bryant, Dwyane Wade or LeBron James were even thought about. His amazing leaping ability and physical stature gave him the physical ability to be an incredible talent on the basketball court. Unfortunately, drugs managed to stop what should have been a promising career.

Bias was a standout at the University of Maryland and voted the nation's top player in 1986. What stood out most about Bias, other than his 6'8" height, was his calm and quiet demeanor. In a world filled with arrogant athletes, the young Bias was considered to be a humble star. His talent and potential was rewarded with a draft selection as the 2nd overall pick to the Boston Celtics in the 1986 NBA draft.

Similar to LeBron James in 2003, Bias was also presented with a multi-million dollar sneaker deal. Yet, a bad choice to use drugs offered from a friend turned fatal for Len Bias. He never had the chance to wear the legendary green Celtics jersey, his signature sneakers or step foot on the infamous "Boston Garden" basketball court.

While attending a party with his college teammate, Len Bias was offered a hit of cocaine from "so called friends." It was said to be his first experiment with drugs. Sadly, the experiment cost him his life. The dose of cocaine eventually sent Bias into convulsions. Two days after being drafted into the NBA, Len Bias was pronounced dead at the age of 22. A young man with unlimited potential and talent was ultimately stopped by an overdose of cocaine.

It is important that you recognize the people around you, from your friends, enemies, and even strangers. Notice how at most playgrounds, you see older people on the side of the playground smoking weed and getting high. What a sad site to see. These people are throwing their lives away. While other people their age are working towards making a better life for themselves, these people spend all their time destroying their own. But what makes it sadder is how they try to get kids to throw their lives away too by participating in the same junk.

Have you ever heard someone yell, "Hey boy, come get some of this!" Instead of getting a job or doing something positive in their community, they'd rather bring it down by getting young kids to throw away their futures. It should be against the law for people like this to hang out around playgrounds or anywhere else where kids play.

When you see old people hanging out smoking and drinking, remember that their life is exactly what it is, THEIR LIFE. It doesn't have to be yours.

Check out the example below.

(Teens at a neighborhood park)

Drugs

Old Man Larry: What up boy? Come get on this "*dro*" with ya boy. You heard what I said? Boy, put that ball down and get a taste of this. It'll get your game real high!

Tim: Man, gone with that man. You know I ain't even with that.

Old Man Larry: Come on boy. This'll get you right!

Tim: Naw, I done already told you. I'm straight.

Remember that you can achieve great things in your lifetime. But if you have negative influences around you like drugs or people who use drugs, chances are that your life will be cut short before you even have a chance to achieve anything. So when someone comes around you talking that MESS, do the best thing possible. The best thing that you can do is to ignore them.

If they keep coming at you with it, then go ahead and check them. Let them know that you aren't down with what they're doing. Make them have enough respect for you to not use around you. When you face someone and let them know where you stand, that shows that you have heart. If they can't respect that, don't respect them. When you see them again, KEEP IT MOVING.

If you have not already figured it out, WEED is a drug. Do you know why people smoke weed? The answer is because they don't have anything better to do. Most people that smoke weed don't have goals or a plan for their future. The only goal they have is to smoke more weed. They use weed as a crutch for others to have sorrow or to make excuses for themselves.

So many people try to show others they are cool because they smoke weed. But you don't have to smoke weed to show people that you're cool. If you even feel you have to show people that you're cool, chances are that you're not! A person is cool through their behavior and actions. There are plenty of people in the game that don't drink nor smoke and they get plenty of RESPECT.

Drugs are not a Solution

A lot of times people use drugs as a solution for their problems. They think that weed or alcohol will solve the problems that they're facing. Wrong! Using drugs won't solve anything.

The only thing drugs will do is make your problems worse. Better yet, drugs will create new problems. When people abuse themselves with drug use, it shows a lack of love. Let's be clear about it.

How can someone really love himself if he is spending his money and time smoking weed all day? That person loves weed more than he loves himself. When you see people drinking "40 ounces" all day, what does that tell you? It should tell you that they don't have love for themselves. You would think that they would use the money to better themselves. Instead, they want to blow money on alcohol. They don't love themselves.

Fall from Stardom

One of the greatest selling rappers of all-time ultimately fell from grace due to the use of drugs. Considered to be one of the biggest rap acts in hip-hop, Earl "DMX" Simmons catapulted onto the rap scene with Ruff Ryders and Def

Jam Records in 1998. At the age of 27, he released his first album *It's Dark and Hell is Hot,* which sold over four million copies.

In 1998, DMX also released his second album *Flesh of My Flesh, Blood of My Blood*, which also sold over four million copies. DMX was as big of a star as anyone from poverty or wealth could have become. Yet, success was not enough to heal the wounds of a damaging childhood.

Earl "DMX" Simmons' upbringing as a child was filled with pain and sorrow. He may have been born to a mother, but he was practically raised in a prison for juvenile offenders. He was introduced to drugs as a teen and eventually began using them as anti-depressants. The internal pain from his childhood never left DMX, even when he reached success through his music. While making millions of fans and achieving stardom, he still found relief in cocaine and marijuana as solutions to problems.

DMX went on to sell over 35 million units of music in his career and even developed a reputation as an actor. He was one of the most in demand stars of the 2000s. But a struggle with cocaine and numerous arrests for marijuana managed to snag DMX from his spotlight. Trouble with the law eventually plagued his shine as a performer and led to frequent jail time. An undercover officer busted him in an attempt to buy cocaine in 2008.

(Teen stands post in a neighborhood filled with crime)

Gettin' Caught Up

One thing about the game is that there are different positions for people to play. Some people think it's cool to use and then there are some of us who view drugs differently. Rather than use them, some see drugs as an opportunity to make cash.

We hear rappers glorify the drug game because of the fast money that comes from it. I won't lie about it; some people can make a quick come up from a product that brings down its customers. Just remember this; what comes easy can be taken even easier.

Selling drugs will never be considered as a career. They don't have retirement plans for drug dealers. People that deal drugs usually don't even make it to see a year of retirement. Even the biggest and most brilliant drug dealers in the world never got away with their crime. Nikki Barnes, Frank Lucas,

George Jung, Rick Ross and so many others made millions in the drug game only to have their freedom seized and incarcerated. Are a few years at the top really worth spending the rest of them down at the bottom?

Is it really worth it to do time in jail because you sold drugs to afford nice clothing and shoes? Is it worth having a permanent bullseye on your back whenever someone looks into your past? You would be better off just getting a legal hustle, such as a job. Why put your future on the line for jewelry and expensive clothes? You'd be better off enlisting in the military.

The life of a former drug dealer is similar to crabs in a barrel. When a crab attempts to climb up the barrel, the other crabs are trying to pull it down. For the rest of your life, people are going to try and keep you down because of your past as a drug dealer. Why put yourself through that when you don't have to?

When you work hard and put in the work you can get what you want in life. Why cheat and try to find the easy way? *Life is a race* and remember that cheaters cannot run forever.

So when you put yourself in the position of moving drugs you have to ask yourself what you should always ask. The question you have to ask is what's more important to you in life? Is it *easy money or control of your future*? When you sell drugs, you have to think of the consequences that come with it.

If the police catch you, the consequence would be *jail time*. If a hater catches you, the consequence could be *a beat down* or even worse, DEATH. A third consequence that some fail to identify is the *loss of morals*. Morals deal with the question of right and wrong. People that sell drugs easily lose morals. They don't understand that what they're doing in their community isn't right, IT'S WRONG.

Giving someone a substance that will abuse them is a cruel form of punishment. In other words, you're helping others destroy their own lives. Their future is in danger because of the pain that you're selling or even offering to them.

So if you decide to start hustling and moving drugs, think first about what you've just read. Then, think to yourself about what's more important in life. Is it *a few dollars* or the *power to have control of your destiny*? No one else can make that decision for you. The answer is for you to decide.

Sometimes we hear rappers talk about selling drugs and we become confused. We begin to think that drug life is something to glamorize. How crazy is that? Let me explain something. People who are "real" drug dealers would NEVER want anyone to know that they are. Back in the day, people were drug dealers because it was a quick way for them to make money. They considered it as a way for them to survive.

Today, people talk about drugs because they want others to think that they are cool. They think that people will respect them if they know that they sell drugs. Do you know what that is? It's corny! If you have to promote drugs to show people that you're cool, chances are that YOU'RE NOT.

Go visit a few prisons in your area. You can find plenty of people that sold drugs. I'm not sure whether they sold drugs to be cool, but I guarantee that they wish they hadn't. Imagine that. Somebody is serving 20 years in jail because they wanted people to think that they're cool. The only problem was that they GOT CAUGHT.

When you think about it, is it really worth it? If you don't think it is, please keep reading. You're reading on towards a great path of wisdom. If you think that it is worth it, PLEASE CLOSE THIS BOOK. Don't even bother reading ahead because you're asleep. Leave this book on a table so that someone else can pick it up.

Life Is A Race

If you have no confidence in self you are twice defeated in the race of life. With confidence you have won even before you have started.

--------Marcus Garvey

If you have ever participated in a marathon you would know how much energy you have to put forth to finish the race. You'll also notice that in a marathon, not everyone who starts will finish.

Some would say that life is like a marathon. Let me break it down just in case you do not agree. In life, you have people that run fast because they want to be the best. Nothing is wrong with running fast, but remember that sometimes when you run too fast you don't have enough energy to finish the race.

Then you have people that run slow because they do not have a desire to be the best. Instead, they're just comfortable with being in the race. They believe that they can't win, so they always run slow.

Then you have another group of runners. These runners don't run too fast, but not too slow. They run the race efficiently because they understand how to run the race. These runners are called pacers. They know that if they run too fast, they won't have enough energy to finish. They also

Life Is A Race

know that if they run too slow, they won't be able to win the race.

Pacers are usually the type of people that win the race. You know why they win? The answer is because they have a plan. They know that in order for them to win they must have a plan of action and they must stick to it.

Another reason why life is considered a race is because like a race, life has winners and losers. Most of us want to be winners in life. Everyday we go out into the world and compete with others to achieve the same goals.

If you are in school, you are competing with your classmates to earn the best grades. When you leave school, you're competing with other students to get into the best colleges. When you graduate from college, you're competing with other graduates to get the best jobs.

When you get a job, you are competing with other employees to get the next promotion. (Some employees will be competing to keep their jobs.) When you finally make it to the top, you're competing with others to stay at the top! See what I mean?

Life is a continuous race. It's like a big competition that runs in a cycle and never stops. The sooner you understand this, the more prepared you'll be for life. People that don't understand this concept are people that end up being beat out by others. That's why it's so important that you learn this at an early age.

Parents that understand the race of life make sure that their kids do to. They do everything possible to send their kids to the best grammar schools available. They make sure that their kids are doing well in school and making good grades. All of this is done for a reason. This reason is because they want their kids to have a head start in the race. They want to make sure that their kids stay ahead of the competition.

Understanding the Game

School provides a great structure for life. The reason why I say this is because you learn so many different things in school. You learn more than just book smarts. You learn how to deal with people, make friends and understand the game.

Understanding the game is one of the most important things you can learn in school. The game is a combination of many things. The game is a combination of how to have fun, fit in, avoid trouble and do well in school.

You would be surprised how much you pick up from the game in school. When the girl that you like turns you down, you learn how to accept rejection. (Hopefully you do.) When your peers try to influence you to use drugs, you learn how to face peer pressure. When you get clowned on for coming to school with a bad haircut, you learn to deal with embarrassment.

When your teacher asks you to be quiet, you learn to respect authority. You develop the skills and learn the things that you need to be successful in the real world. Once you know how to play the game, you'll be considered as balanced.

A lot of kids that do not have good training at home end up "mentally challenged" later on in life. Those kids are the ones who can't make passing grades in their classes or read on the level that they are required to. The goal for elementary school is to prepare you and start you on the right track.

By the time you get to the 3rd grade, you should be able to read and write at the normal level. But for some reason there are always some students who just can't keep up. These students end up being separated from the other students in the class who perform well.

Kids who cannot perform well are separated and place under the title, "*slow*." The kids who perform well are placed in the category, "*accelerated*." Think about this. If you're placed in the slow lane at the very beginning, how could you possibly catch up to the students who are "*accelerated*?"

Ever wonder why you see some kids stuck in the same grade longer than others? They become comfortable with being in the "slow" lane. The only way they can be motivated to catch up to their peers is if you place them in the same race.

There is no reason why a 13-year old should be in the 5th grade! There are even some cases where a 16-year old is in the 6th grade or 7th grade! Eventually, some kids get to the point to where they can't "pass" to the next grade, so they get "promoted." The difference between pass and promotion is that when you pass, you've earned the right to go to the next grade. A student gets promoted because they have become too old to remain in the same grade.

The disadvantage of social promotion is that it remains with students permanently. Even when they get older, they're still getting promoted. They get promoted for the same reason that they did in school, because they can't remain in the same position for too long. In a way, you could call being promoted as "being cheated."

Cheaters cannot run forever

Then there are people that believe they cannot win unless they find an advantage. The only problem with this is that their way of finding an advantage is by "cheating." Don't act like you don't know what I'm talking about.

No matter what class you are in, there is always one student that just has to cheat. Whether it's a test or a paper, that person just can't *come correct*. Instead of giving their brain a chance to learn, they'd rather find a way to cheat. Some people are so good at cheating, they could teach a class about it!

Believe it or not, but there are people that have cheated their way all through school. Some people have even cheated through college! I'm not sure how they did it, but it's been done. The thing about cheaters is that they start at an early age.

Check out this example.

> **Steve**: Hey Duane, you ready for that test in Mr. Brown's class.
>
> **Duane**: You know me. I'm always ready.
>
> *Duane quietly shows Steve a small piece of paper from his pocket.*
>
> **Steve**: I see you got your help with you. You shouldn't even need it. Mr. Brown reviewed the test last week and he stayed after class all this week to go over and prepare us for the test.
>
> **Duane**: What? Man, I'm not trying to hear that. I've got all the preparation I need right in my pocket.

People that work hard for their achievements usually stay at the top or they climb even higher. The people that may not have worked hard to get where they are usually end up falling down, FAST. For example, in the late 80's and early 90's there were two guys from Germany that considered themselves as entertainers. They decided to go by the name Milli Vanilli.

In 1988, Milli Vanilli came out with an album titled *Girl You Know It's True*. Several songs off the album became hits across the world. Their most successful single, *Girl You Know It's True*, became a pop smash. Everybody knew the words to that song. The song became so successful that they won a Grammy award in 1990 for *Best New Artist*.

It was as if nothing could stop Milli Vanilli. It was as if their career was too good to be true. Unfortunately, there was something that not only stopped them, but also exposed them to the world. What eventually ended their success was THE TRUTH. They couldn't sing!

In fact, Milli Vanilli never sung any of the songs on the album that helped them receive a Grammy. They did what is now called "lip singing" at all of their previous performances. The industry and their audience labeled them as "jokes" once it was known that they never sung on any of their songs.

The Grammy award won by Milli Vanilli was revoked that same year after the shocking news was released. Eventually, they were dropped from their label. Their album and their masters were deleted from the catalog of Arista Records.

People who were once fans demanded refunds for the purchase of Milli Vanilli's album and concert tickets. All of this humiliation could have been prevented if Milli Vanilli had taken their time to develop their natural ability instead of cutting corners and cheating.

Cheating only leaves the door open for you to be exposed later on. The sporting world is filled with people who thought they could maneuver around the rules of the game. Baseball greats Barry Bonds, Mark McGuire, Jose Canseco and Alex Rodriguez are just a few of the hundreds of athletes who chose to cheat. Former female track sensation Marion Jones was ultimately stripped of her gold medals and titles when discovered she had used banned substances. Even colleges are exposed every year for violating the rules when recruiting the top players to their athletic programs.

Cheating is really no different from stealing. Instead of working and proving yourself, a cheater chooses to steal his victory. True champions want to earn the crown, rather than steal it.

Cheaters will never understand that a real win or *achievement* can never be scammed. A win only has meaning when you earn it. Any accolade or recognition won by someone who did not rightfully earn it is only a *"cheaterment."* It means nothing.

Do NOT get left behind

The one thing that you definitely do not want to do is fall behind in the race of life. The reason why is because once you fall behind, you have to work twice as hard to get to the front. Usually when you're in the back, people that won't win the race surround you.

What is worse is that those people in the back probably will not even finish the race. Then, they'll try to trap you into their way of thinking. Soon you'll believe that you won't finish the race.

Most people that end up in the back of the race end up dead or in jail. The people in front of the race end up becoming successful and live on to enjoy their success. What you have to decide is where do you want to be in this race? Is it in the back or in the front? The actions that you take and the choices that you make will decide where you'll be.

The world is filled with people who are disciplined and understand that the race is filled with competitors. Winners recognize that if they want to be successful they too must become disciplined and competitive. That's why they come to class on time and do their work until their tasks are completed. When I say on time, I mean *early*. They understand the importance of being *prompt*.

As young people, we must adapt some of these same principles if we want to achieve excellence in the race of life. If we're supposed to come to school at 7:30 a.m., we need to be prepared so that we can be on time. Some of us won't even leave the house until 7:30 a.m. How crazy is that! It's as if we don't have priorities for ourselves.

When you are tardy, it shows others that you have a lack of respect for time. More importantly, it shows people that you have a lack of respect for their time. Believe it or not, but everyone recognizes your ignorance and tardiness, from friends, teachers and eventually employers. It's almost impossible to win with this negative habit. Check out this example of when tardiness goes wrong.

(Gary goes through a life of being late, from childhood to adulthood.)

Gary before school

Mama: Gary, get your butt up! It's almost 7:00am and you're gonna be late for school again!

Gary during school

Ms. Brown: Gary, it's now five minutes into class and you're just now walking in. I'm sending you to the dean's office for detention this week.

Gary after school

Sheila: Where have you been Gary! You were supposed to meet me at the library an hour ago.

That's the last time you'll disrespect me. Don't call my phone again!

Gary in college

Professor Rollins: Gary, you know the rules. Three tardies and you fail my class. I'll see you again next semester.

Gary at work

Mr. Johnson: Gary it seems as if you have a problem coming to work on time. Fortunately for us, it's no longer our problem. We're going to have to let you go. We can no longer tolerate your tardiness. You're fired.

Do you see how something so simple to others is a big problem for some of us? Being late ended up ruining Gary's life. Let this story be a lesson for you to learn from. You cannot win in the race of life if you're constantly late for everything. Instead you will lose.

<u>*Where are you in the race of life?*</u>

Winners:

1. Respect authority
2. Are responsible for their actions
3. Make sure that tasks are done right
4. Do their best at all times
5. Complete what they start
6. Have a plan

Losers:

Life Is A Race

1. Use drugs
2. Make excuses
3. Are always tardy
4. Don't listen
5. Give up easily
6. Act without thinking

Life is about who makes it, not who makes it the fastest.
---- Clifford "T. I." Harris

Get Educated

A mayor can give you a key to the city. A desire for education will give you a key to the world. An education should be considered as the master key to any locked door leading to success.

-- Ivan James

Outside of religion, an education is the one valuable that no one can steal from you. Someone can steal a car, money, or a girlfriend. One thing that cannot be stolen is an education.

Having knowledge will allow you to travel as far as you want to go. You might come from the worst neighborhood in the city, but good grades can get you a scholarship to any place or school you choose. An education can be your escape route from the streets or any negative environment.

Your crossover on the basketball court or speed on the football field are not the only ways to escape poverty. Making good grades in the classroom is even more of a guarantee that you'll rise above poor surroundings. A knee injury can jeopardize a career in basketball and football, but nobody can injure your mind. A NFL team can cut you from a team at the end of a season, but an education will always give you an option for employment.

When you think about it, the two things that are taught free of charge are religion and education. Beginning at the age of five, the government provides a free education to you for 13 years. You decide if the free education will continue beyond those 13 years based on your GPA and what scores you achieve on standardized testing.

There are people in this world who have went from Kindergarten to Law School free of charge because their academic performance earned scholarships that paid for them to continue their education. Your education can be paid in full if you choose to work hard and earn good grades.

Education is life-changing

A great example of the power of education can be found in the life of Ben Carson. Growing up on the streets of Detroit, Ben and his brother were raised in a single parent home. Poverty couldn't even begin to define the struggles that young Ben, his brother and mother went through. Education would become Ben Carson's escape route, but it didn't come easy.

Ben performed terribly in school and was considered "the dummy of the class." Known for his violent temper, poverty and difficulty in the classroom seemed to have Ben's future already decided. However, his mother refused to allow him to give up. She forced him to read two books a week and write book reports after reading each one. The task of reading books eventually became an enjoyment.

Books allowed Ben to remove his mind from being poor and allowed his imagination to take him anywhere. He realized that living in poverty was temporary and that he had the power to change his situation. Reading developed a desire in Ben to learn more. His grades improved dramatically, as well as his confidence. He finished grade school as the top student of an all-white institution and later graduated from high school with honors.

Ben Carson's desire to learn took him to Yale University. He earned a degree in psychology and went on to enroll in the School of Medicine at the University of Michigan. With great eye-hand coordination, Ben became a great surgeon.

He eventually received an invitation for a neurosurgeon position in Perth, Australia. The desire for education took him from poverty in the inner city to places all across the world. Not bad for someone who was once considered the class dummy.

The first step to excelling is to make your education a top priority. This means setting time aside each day to study and better yourself. Make an effort to improve in subjects that you may struggle in. If math has always been tough, find extra time to focus on it. Never allow what you don't know prevent you from moving ahead.

Ask Questions

One of the most common ways to get educated is to always ask questions. Never be afraid to ask a question if there's something you do not know. You should never feel like your question is stupid no matter what you ask. The dumbest questions are only the ones that never get asked. Remember that no one knows it all. At some point everyone needs help at something.

What prevents us from asking for help is our fear of how we are viewed. Asking a question in front of our peers makes us seem like we are dumb and inferior. This way of thinking is a setback in getting educated. The person that is brave enough to ask a question is the same person that has what it takes to succeed in life; confidence. It takes confidence to ask for help.

Having confidence allows you to step out of your comfort zone and do whatever it takes to prepare for success.

Cowards are those who stay quiet when they desperately need help in their studies. Confident people are those who decide to take action and let nothing or no one stand in their way to get educated. Ask yourself, which one are you?

How far do you think you'll go in life without asking questions and becoming educated? Don't keep quiet when it comes to your education. Be confident and take charge!

Education increases the odds

Having an education is what increases your percentage of being successful within the world. There are people in the world that reached success without a college degree, but those individuals should be considered as exceptions. As you read this book, even you might reach success without ever going to college. You should still keep in mind that you will face your peers each day for jobs that you want. An education will only make you that much more appealing to the world.

Even if you desire to be your own boss and start a business, an education should be considered as your launching pad. I say this because most people seeking to start a business will need a business plan and startup capital. Unless you have money stashed in an abandoned house or bank in Mexico, you are definitely going to need startup capital. This means that you will have to apply for a loan from a bank or convince others to invest. Don't you think that an education can help aid you in this process? It will certainly show that you have the ability to finish what you plan to start.

Education gives you options

Just as when a young man begins to date, it is always best when you give yourself options. You should never limit yourself. Choosing to stick with one person for a long-time will not give you any kind of back-up plan. An education can be viewed the same way. Without a high level of knowledge, you are considered limited.

An education should be viewed as a way to increase your options. In basketball, you can never expect to win a championship without options. Kobe Bryant was the best player in basketball for several years, but he wasn't able to win a title until he had options on his team. Players like Paul Gasol and Lamar Odom became other scoring options that teams had to defend. With options, the Lakers became a devastating force and eventually won multiple NBA championships. The Lakers organization received praise because they provided options around their superstar, Kobe Bryant.

In fact, athletes and entertainers should be the primary individuals seeking to educate themselves with as much knowledge as possible. A businessman's mouth salivates like a fat kid at a pizza party the moment they see someone with the potential to be a money maker, not to mention a young minority. They prey on potential money makers from the day the public shows an interest. For close to two decades, the number one source for potential money makers was a high school gymnasium.

From High School to the NBA

Before the NBA enforced their minimum age rule in 2006, going to college was almost considered as a negative. High school ballplayers would only go to college if they were unsure that an NBA team would select them. A player who would have benefited greatly from the minimum age rule would have been Chicago native, Eddy Curry.

Eddy Curry was a lottery pick in the 2001 NBA Draft and selected by none other than the Chicago Bulls. The

18-year old became an instant millionaire. His expenses immediately shot up through the roof from buying cars and homes. It was as if he had an unlimited payroll and sharing his riches with others became second nature.

Almost 10 years later, Eddy Curry found himself as an injured reserve missing the majority of every season in his career. Gambling debts and high expenses forced Eddy to file for a loan with an 80% interest rate! Mobsters and loan sharks wouldn't even apply an 80% interest rate for a loan! What's even worse is that he is struggling to overcome debt.

Many may not believe it, but going to college may have curbed some of the bad financial decisions that Curry made. A college financial accounting course would have taught the 6'11" center his accounts receivable, accounts payable, checks and balances, as well as the basics in starting up a small business.

Anyone seeking a career in sports and entertainment should at least take a personal finance course somewhere within their journey. You should have an interest in learning how to manage your own money. Understand what it takes to budget your income and expenses rather than look for someone to do it for you.

People have no idea how many business managers seek to rip off their clients and steal money from them. You can never expect others to look out for your best interest until you first take the initiative to look out for yourself. Get educated!

It would even be wise to take a course in investments. That way once you begin to make the big bucks you'll know how to properly invest your money. An entrepreneurship course would also be a wise class to enroll in. This will teach you the components of a business plan, as well as how profits are generated in a business.

The moment you receive big bucks people are going to come from all over with business plans urging you to invest. Wouldn't it be a good idea to understand how to read one first? The majority of businesses fail to remain in business after their first year. Knowing what to look for in a business plan may save you time, money and peace of mind.

Former NBA All-Star Antoine Walker made over $110 million dollars in his NBA career. Two years after his last game with the Minnesota Timberwolves, Antoine was forced to file bankruptcy in 2010. How in the world does someone go bankrupt after earning such a fortune? Even with Uncle Sam snatching half the money from Walker's pocket, $55 million is still more money than 90% of the world will ever see.

Education equals Qualification

Believe it or not, but the world can be a difficult place when you lack education. The impact of technology has completely dominated how we live, work and communicate with each other. Technology has also made it more competitive when seeking jobs. The days of walking into an office with a resume are non-existent. People prefer that you apply for a job on-line rather than meet you face to face.

The two things that stick out the most on any resume are experience and education. You might be the nicest person in the world, but the only thing that people want to know is if you are educated. Your level of education will place you into two categories: qualified and unqualified. If you're qualified, then you become compared only to others who are also considered qualified. If you're not qualified, then you get overlooked and eventually dismissed.

When you are seeking a job in the real world, chances are you will need a college degree. The world today is filled with so many people competing for the same positions that you need a college degree to even be considered. A high school diploma barely gets you a shot at a good job. A college degree once guaranteed the best wages available, but now a degree only gets you into the game.

In order to give yourself the best chance to succeed, consider getting advanced degrees or the highest level of education needed to shine in the career you plan to pursue. Not to say that you can't make it with just a college degree, because people have made it to the top with just a high school diploma. Yet, advanced degrees can save you a lot of time on your way up the ladder of success.

Like a track runner, you want to come out of the blocks in front of the pack. The best way to give yourself that advantage is by getting the best education possible.

Taking Charge of your Education

If a parent can cough up $200 a week to send their kid to basketball camp, then that same parent should be able to afford for their child to visit a tutor at least once a week. Parents just have to have their priorities in order. Regardless of race or background, intelligence and the thirst for knowledge should be encouraged within every household. There's no reason for any student to accept grades that are below average when there are tutors and learning centers that volunteer their time.

Regardless of how difficult a class may be, we must make an effort to take advantage of our resources. Instead of purchasing the latest video game, put some money into a tutoring session. Why put money into a video game or some source of entertainment when you are suffering in your schoolwork?

Instead of giving your money to the game developers

who already have millions of dollars, why don't you put that money into your education? What sense does it make to spend money on what we don't need when our education is at stake? Come on THINK!

We just have to decide what is more important to us. Do we desire to have the best clothing and shoes? Do we desire to have the best education? If we can manage to spend over $100 for a pair of sneakers, why can't we afford to buy the Texas Instruments calculator needed in our mathematics class? If we can spend over $40 for a shirt, why do we say we cannot afford to buy the required textbook for our class? We can never expect for an education to hold value until we make an effort to obtain one.

An education may not be as important during your present. Yet, it can have a dominant effect on you in your future. Give yourself the best chance to succeed in your future by doing what is required of you in the classroom.

Better yet, do "more" than what is required of you in the classroom. Make it your responsibility to take the lead in your schoolwork. Develop the habit of reviewing material until you understand it well enough to explain to another student.

Another way to take charge in your education is to remain motivated to be the best in your class. If there is a student that is making better grades than you, challenge yourself to top that student. No matter whom they are or how much money their family has, a person has no edge over you in the classroom. You can work just as hard and outshine anybody if you desire to excel in your studies.

Smart students review the course syllabus and read the required material before the school semester even starts! They'll study and attempt to learn the material on their own. By the time the school semester begins, they appear to be

Get Educated

geniuses and light-years ahead of everyone else. We come to start off the year without a clue of what is even about to take place in our class. Yet, we stay *clean* and *draped* from head to toe in the latest clothing.

The reason those other students might run circles around us in the classroom is because of a key ingredient that is required in anything related to success. The reason others appear more intelligent and we do not is because of their preparation and our lack thereof. To become prepared, one must also take initiative.

Take it upon yourself to study, rather than only studying when someone tells you to. There's no reason to wait until the last minute to study or complete an assignment if you were aware of it in advance. That's not preparation. That is called desperation.

In what rulebook does it say that you can only open your textbook when your teacher tells you to in class? If your class grade were at stake, wouldn't you want to open that textbook and review the material as much as possible? We wait until we hear of a test before it sinks in our head to take notes.

Choosing to sit back and wait for someone else to tell you to study is only an example of laziness. We should never be lazy when it comes to education. You can never expect to get ahead if you're constantly trying to catch up.

Our young people must understand this concept and become encouraged to not slack off or ease up in the classroom. The sooner you can grasp this concept, the sooner you can step on the gas pedal and accelerate towards receiving the best education possible.

The primary key to excelling in your studies and becoming educated comes from preparation. You can never expect to perform at a high level unless you take the time to prepare yourself. Do you think that basketball legend

Michael Jordan could have dominated on the basketball court without putting in ample time in practice?

Do you think that football great Peyton Manning could have ever reached the level of greatness that he achieved without putting in hours of practice and even more hours of film review? The same principle applies when it comes to our education. Our preparation determines the results that we receive. What you learn establishes the grades that you earn.

Education can predict your future

What our young people must realize as quickly as possible is that an education eventually dictates our positions later in life. For the majority of us who won't make it to the NBA, NFL, NHL, MLB or become a famous entertainer, chances are we will have to pursue a more general career. Your performance in the classroom can determine how everything else in your life will turn out.

The way you perform in grade school dictates the type of classes you'll take in high school. Good students are placed in honors and Advanced Placement (AP) classes. Failing students find themselves in remedial classes. Mediocre students find themselves somewhere in the mix.

Eventually, good high school students are awarded scholarships to colleges and universities. Mediocre students may end up at City College or a Junior College. Failing students find themselves slipping through the cracks. Some immediately join the work force and struggle to live off the minimum wage salary that they earn due to a lack of education. Others may not even work at all and put their time to use by breaking the law.

Ultimately, good college students graduate and

are awarded with well-paying jobs that allow them the opportunity to live a good lifestyle. Those mediocre students become employees in positions that may not pay so well, while they struggle to provide for themselves or their families. Sadly, the students who were once failing in grade school are now serving time for criminal activities because no one would hire them since they were considered unqualified. Each outcome was determined based on the effort put forth from day one in the grade school classroom.

The best way to encourage you to take charge of your education can be derived from the scenario described above. Choosing not to work hard in your schoolwork can result in you becoming one of those failing students headed for trouble. You don't have to go out like that. Why choose to make life more difficult when all you have to do is focus and work hard in school? Take charge of your education so that you can provide yourself with the best opportunities available.

The right academic history can get you into any school you want for free. Colleges and universities will flood your mailbox requesting for you to apply to their school. Students with average grades and scores end up having to take alternative routes, along with paying for education through student loans.

Those students with a poor academic history are backed into a corner and have to take even more alternatives. Community and junior college ends up being their only option. Don't limit yourself if you don't have to. Get off your ass and take charge of your education.

Take Notes:

Having an education can never hurt, but only help you.

Athletes and entertainers should be the first to seek an education.

Have an interest in learning how to manage your own money.

Never expect for others to look out for your best interest unless you take the initiative to get educated.

(Education)

Which subjects give you the most difficulty? What extra steps do you intend to make so that you can overcome the challenges you face with complex classes?

What subjects do you excel the most in?

What careers or professions are directly related to the subjects that you mostly excel in?

What colleges or universities offer programs directly related to the career or profession you intend to pursue?

What are the eligibility requirements for enrollment into each college or university?

What scholarships are available? What are the requirements to receive each scholarship?

Plan = Goals + Steps

A lot of times it seems like you ain't gonna make it where you wanna be in life, but if you gotta plan believe me you gonna get there. You gonna get everything you ever wanted. That's my word.

----Nasir "Nas" Jones
The Lost Tapes

The biggest problem for us as young people is that we do not plan for our future. We think too much about today, instead of planning ahead for tomorrow. To break it down, think about it like this. When you have a test in a class, you have two ways that you can prepare for it. You can study early and prepare or you can cram the night before the test.

Guess which people will do the best when it's time to take the test? You shouldn't even have to guess because you know the people that studied and prepared early will be the ones that do the best. This is the same way that life works out. Those that work hard and plan ahead have the best chances at being successful.

Society makes us believe that as minorities we do not have what it takes to be a success. Think about it. In school or in group projects, students are always trying to pair up with the white guy or girl because they assume that they are smarter.

This same attitude follows us into adulthood. We see

white people doing well and we assume that it's because they're smarter. In actuality, we need to focus on preparing ourselves and making sure that we have what's most important, A PLAN.

Create a plan for anything that you want to do in life. The purpose of having a plan is so that you'll always know your ultimate goal. Your plan will help you reach your ultimate goal by establishing objectives.

Objectives are smaller goals that help you progress towards reaching your ultimate goal. Once you've set your objectives, you're ready to write out the steps that you need to take to reach your objectives. Let me break it down for you.

If your ultimate goal is to play in the NBA, then your first objective should be to make your high school basketball team. The steps to help you make the high school basketball team are knowing your fundamentals, developing your ability to play good defense, practicing drills and having the positive attitude of a team player. *Remember that some of the best basketball players in the world will never make it to the NBA because they don't know how to play with the team.*

Ultimate Goal

- NBA

First Objective

- Make your high school basketball team.

Steps

1. Know your fundamentals.

Plan = Goals + Steps

2. Work on your defense.
3. Master your basketball drills.
4. Have a team first mentality.

Do you understand the importance of a plan? Lets look at another example in case you are still confused.

If your ultimate goal is to be an entertainer, you need to know all of the options that are available to entertainers. Your first objective should be to get involved in as many events as possible, so that you can showcase your talent. You should know what events are going to happen in the future. Another step would be to network with others who are involved in events and learn how you can impact each event.

Ultimate Goal
- To be an entertainer.

First Objective
- Get involved in as many events as possible.

Steps
1. Know what events are taking place in the future.
2. Network with others who are involved in events.
3. Learn how you can impact each event.

Remember that in the race of life, sometimes you have to go the extra mile to achieve your goals. If you want to earn an A in a difficult class, the extra mile may be that you'll have to study with other students that understand the class material. Let me break it down for you.

Ultimate Goal
- Earn an A in a difficult class.

First Objective
- Earn an A on the first test.

Steps
1. Read the assigned material.
2. Do your homework.
3. Ask questions if you're confused.

Extra Mile
- Study with other students that understand the class material.

Once you have developed a plan, you will realize that everything in life requires a plan of action. From your goals to your career, you need to have a plan in place. Yeah you heard right, A CAREER.

Young students must realize that they need to figure out what type of career they want to pursue. A lot of us don't think about it while we're in school, but it'll bite you in the butt later on in life. People that don't have a plan usually end up in one of three places: dead, jail, or living with their mama.

The last thing you want in life is to be 30 years old and living at your mama's house. That's why it's important that you have some type of plan for your life. Believe it or not, some students actually go away to college just to get away from home. It may sound silly, but they at least had a PLAN. Even though they don't know what they want to be or what they want to major in, they at least had a plan to get out of their mama's house.

Even if you do not know exactly what you want to be

yet, it's OKAY. It's hard to know exactly what you want to be. But you do need to understand what you're good at. Once you figure out what you are good at, it will become easier to establish what you want to do.

When you figure out what you are good at, you can then find out if you can develop it into a career. Once you discover if there's a career that matches what you like to do, figure out the requirements and see if you meet them. If you don't meet the requirements right away, determine how you can. Remember that if this is something that you want to pursue, you'll have to do whatever is necessary to MAKE IT HAPPEN.

Once you know the requirements for the career you want to pursue, see if there are any opportunities that are available. If you don't see any right away, keep looking. Don't give up and settle for just a job. Remember that a job is something that people have so that they can get by in life. A career allows you to earn an income while doing something that you enjoy and are qualified to do.

Job – something that people have to get by in life.

Career – allows you to earn an income while doing something that you enjoy and are qualified to do.

Finding your career:
1. Find out what you are good at.
2. From the list of things that you're good at, decide on what you enjoy doing.
3. Find out what types of careers are associated with what you're good at.

4. Identify the requirements to pursue each career.
5. Identify the opportunities that are associated with each career.
6. Decide which career you want to pursue.

Your plan is one of the most important tools for your future. You should consider your plan as a blueprint for success. Know that the people that have a plan for their life usually succeed. The reason why is because they took time to develop a strategy. It wasn't as if they just did things and everything worked out. Like I said before, they had a strategy.

A Master Plan with *No Limit*

Percy "Master P" Miller was raised in one of the most violent housing projects in New Orleans, Louisiana. Despite harsh surroundings, he had a plan to develop one of the most successful brands in entertainment. Business courses completed in college and a $10,000.00 settlement, led the young Miller to open a small record store.

Master P had a vision to develop and release music under his own record label. At a time when hip hop was dominated by the East and West coasts, the thought of launching a successful New Orleans rap label sounded impossible. Still, Master P believed in his vision to release his own albums and created a plan to support it.

During that time period, the release of an album was based on radio airplay. Depending upon the radio popularity of a single, listeners would determine if a major label would invest in promoting an album or not release it. Master P had his own strategy. Rather than depend on airtime from radio, he chose to independently promote his music on the streets and sell tapes from the trunk of his car. For three

Plan = Goals + Steps

years, Master P maintained a profitable rate of album sales without the help of any major record company.

The key to the success of his independent label was to provide more music per album than his competition. Mainstream albums at that time only had 10 to 14 songs. Master P would provide up to 20 songs and longer play time for the same price.

By 1997, No Limit Records was home to several artists who managed to build solid fan bases. He was rewarded a distribution deal with Priority Records due to the success of the independent label. The deal gave No Limit Records nationwide distribution while allowing Master P to expand the No Limit name into other ventures.

The next step in Master P's plan was the release of a movie. With no financial support or interest from major film companies, Master P chose to finance the film on his own. He produced, directed, financed and starred in his first movie, *I'm Bout It*. The straight to video movie sold over 200,000 copies within five weeks of its release, while the movie's soundtrack went platinum. The success from the independent release of *I'm Bout It* was rewarded with a distribution deal through Dimension Films for the release of his next movie.

Within a year, Master P went forth with his next step and began the operation for new No Limit ventures. He started a sports management firm, sneaker and clothing lines, an exclusive film production company, travel agency and several other businesses. No Limit was no longer just a record label. It was now a brand. Master P fulfilled his mission to make No Limit one of the most dominant enterprises of the 90's.

Plan to create an entertainment empire

1. Trademark company logo.

2. Create music that appeals to your target audience.
3. Use profits from music sales to develop films catered to your target audience.
4. Use profits from music and film sales to expand the company brand with new ventures that also appeal to your target audience .

Keys to Master P's plan

1. Avoid borrowing; Take profit from one venture and invest in the next.
2. Eliminate the middle man as much as possible.
3. Cross promote your products.
4. Aim to give what your customers want.

A plan shows people that you have put thought into what you hope to achieve. When you take the time to write down a strategy, you show others that you are serious. It's so easy today for people to talk about what they plan to do. But how many people actually write down how they plan to do it?

As I described earlier in this chapter, look at having a plan as preparation for a test. Imagine yourself taking a test you know you didn't study for. What kind of grade do you think you'll score? Now imagine taking that same test, except this time you studied and prepared for it. Now what grade do you think you'll score? I'm pretty sure you'll score a whole lot better than you would without studying. This is the way you should look at having a plan.

Having a plan shows that you have studied and prepared yourself for the future. People that don't have a plan are viewed as walking into life unprepared. Now do you

Plan = Goals + Steps

understand why so many people become failures? They have no plan.

You cannot just wake up every morning and expect for your life to just fall into place. You might be able to get away with it while you're young, but it will catch up with you in the long run. It's only so long before mama kicks your butt out of the house. If she doesn't, please believe that she's not doing you a favor. No one over the age of 24 should still be living with their parents. The only thing you'll grow up to become is "crippled."

Just as Denzel Washington said as Coach Boone in *Remember the Titans*, "the world won't take it easy on you, especially if you're black." Sooner or later, you'll have to face the real world and all the challenges that come along with it. Don't you think that having a plan will help? Give yourself the advantage. Don't wait until it's too late. Make it happen. Make your plan today!

Take Notes:

In life there are so many roads that will come along your way. Don't allow yourself to get confused. Make a plan so that you'll have the right directions to follow.

What are your current goals?

How do you plan to achieve these goals?

What are your future goals?

How do you plan to achieve your long-term goals?

Go Get Yours

(Author Ivan James with multi-media executive Kevin Liles)

(Author Ivan James with entrepreneur and media mogul Russell Simmons)

Believe----Achieve----Succeed-----Reflect

I remember in my neighborhood, I used to tell guys I was going to be a professional football player or basketball player and they used to laugh. I used to always say that my mom said I could do anything I wanted. And it was like a joke to them. Well, I'm not laughing at them now, but now I'm the one doing the laughing.

----Allen Iverson

Believe in YOU

Throughout school and life, people are going to question your abilities. These people could be your friends, teachers, classmates, teammates, coaches, and *even parents*. Just remember that you must believe in YOU. It's not important whether or not others believe in your potential. Your ultimate success will be based on whether or not you believe in how great a person you are.

In life, we all want people to support us in our goals and dreams. The reason why we want to be supported is because we care about what others think of us. If your friends tell you that your shoes look corny, it makes you believe that your shoes are corny.

No matter how old you get, people will always want to

feel accepted by others. As kids, we want friends to accept us and our parents to be proud of us. There's nothing wrong with that.

Being accepted is a goal that we all want to achieve. Just make sure that your friends and your peers accept you for being you. If your friends can't accept you the way you are, chances are those are not your friends.

One way you can find out if your friends are real friends is by how supportive they are of you. Some of us have people that we believe are our friends because we talk with them all the time. But notice when you talk with them if they're always laughing about your problems. It's a shame how some people can find humor from the mistakes or misfortunes of others. Even some of the people that we think are our friends can fall to such a low level. Here's an example below.

Chris: Aye Sean, did you pass the final exam in Mr. Wright's Algebra class?

Mitch: Yeah Sean, you've been studying for two weeks straight.

Sean: Naw, I didn't pass. Since I failed the class, I'll have to take it this summer.

Mitch smirks at Chris. Chris smirks back at Mitch.

Chris (grinning): Oh, that's too bad.

What makes our society crazy is the fact that there are actually people in the world that feel good to see you fail at something. Not only is that crazy, but it's sick. Think about it. How can you laugh about watching someone else's vision crumble? Sadly, there are people out there that really enjoy it. If you are one of those people, please try to break that cycle of hatred.

Supporting the misfortunes and downfalls of others will not benefit you nor motivate you to achieve the goals that you have set for yourself. What it will do is show others how much of a wicked person you are. Better yet, it shows how EVIL you are. When people see that, no one will try to help you achieve your goals neither.

Lose Yourself

Marshall "Eminem" Mathers a.k.a. Slim Shady came out with a hit song in 2004 called, *"Lose Yourself."* This song was released as the theme for Eminem's critically acclaimed film, *8 Mile. "Lose Yourself"* contained probably some of the best lyrics you could ever find for motivation. "Success is my only option, failure's not" is probably the most valuable quote of the entire song.

Eminem's quote from *"Lose Yourself"* is the pure definition of a person that believes he will become successful. If you do not allow yourself to fail, then there's no way that you cannot succeed. Keep your mind only on success and never allow yourself to even develop the thought of failure. Doubt should never live inside of you. The term "failure" should not even exist to you.

The belief that you have in yourself is no different from faith. You must always believe that you can do anything that you put your mind to. The moment you doubt yourself is the moment that you begin to prepare for failure. Instead of working towards progress, you're already beginning to expect the worst. No one can reach the top without first believing in themselves. Lose yourself into only achieving your dream.

The story of the urban fashion line FUBU is an example of how far you can go when you lose yourself in your vision. FUBU was originally just a hat line. The success of selling hats could have been enough for most people, but young CEO Daymond John believed that it could become much more. He and his partners chose to stop playing it safe and expand their brand and their vision. Right out his mother's basement with neighborhood friends, he launched FUBU in Queens, NY.

The four friends shared in Daymond John's vision of making and marketing clothing exclusively for the hip-hop culture. They developed designs for T-shirts, jeans, hats and even hockey jerseys. Yet, the company struggled to market their clothing the way fashion designers traditionally marketed fashion lines. Rather than get discouraged, Daymond John and his crew believed in their dream. Their belief was too strong to allow anything or anyone stop their mission.

The young men believed in their vision so much that they made believers out of performers who represented the culture FUBU targeted. Team FUBU ultimately chose to recruit hip-hop artists that identified and believed in their brand, "For Us By Us." LL Cool J was one of the most notable entertainers that heavily endorsed FUBU.

The company began to develop a heavy presence within hip-hop and FUBU eventually became a household name. FUBU went on to revolutionize the industry and stamped their name as one of the biggest trendsetters in urban fashion. Not bad for a company that originated in the basement at big momma's house.

Stop Caring about what everyone Thinks

One thing you need to realize is that life is too short to worry about how others view you. In other words, don't waste time caring about what others think about you. If you have an idea or a goal set for yourself, then it shouldn't matter if someone else thinks it's stupid. What's important is what you think.

There are people today that have spent their whole life worrying about what someone else thinks about them. Now that's stupid. How can you be a grown man walking around trying to please everyone? What should be most important to you in your life is making sure that you're pleased with yourself.

The worst thing that you can do is to allow someone else to crush the goals that you have set. Instead of accepting their criticism and comments, stand up for your goals. Take control of your destiny, rather than wait for someone else to approve it.

Do you think Barack Obama would have made it to the White House had he not had the utmost confidence and believed in himself? Who could have ever predicted that we would one day have an African-American become the President of the United States? His monumental achievement was made possible because he never allowed anyone to shatter his dream.

Imagine a black teenager in Chicago in the late 1970s talking about how he is going to one day become President of the USA. People probably laughed every time they saw him coming their way. To hear a black man talk about one day entering politics, let alone land in the White House was heard only in a comedy routine from Richard Pryor. Still, Barack never stopped believing in what he could accomplish.

While everyone else was laughing, Barack Obama was putting in work. He graduated with a law degree from Harvard and came back to serve in the city of Chicago. His hard work within the city allowed Obama the necessary experience and support to hold a seat in the Senate.

In 2006, Barack Obama began the groundwork for his Presidential campaign by traveling all over the country speaking to citizens in every state. He believed in his vision so much that citizens all over the United States began to believe in him. Two years later, America showed just how much they believed in him by voting him in as the President of the United States. Imagine how many people had to pick their faces off the ground?

Actions Speak Louder than Words

Sometimes we want others to support us in our goals and dreams. We feel that if they believe in us then we will also believe in ourselves. It's similar to how a coach motivates his team to work hard. He tells his players to put forth 100% at all times.

From childhood to adulthood, we all want someone to encourage and push us from time to time. But in life it doesn't always work that way. In life, more people will knock you for what you're trying to do, rather than support you. Don't be fooled, but don't be afraid either. You can overcome this with a simple rule. Rather than tell everyone your visions, let people see your actions.

When others see how hard you work and how dedicated you are, you won't have to tell people your goals. Instead, they'll recognize them from the work that you've put in. Once your peers see how much work you put into achieving your goals, they won't just recognize you; they'll respect you.

Fear ~ Failure

Another obstacle that sometimes stands in our way to achieving our goals is our fear of failure. Some of us are just too afraid to make a mistake. No one in the world enjoys making mistakes in life. But in order to succeed, sometimes you have to make a few errors.

Errors help you to learn what not to do the next time you attempt to achieve that same goal. Errors can even help you remember what not to do when you attempt other goals. I guess you could say that errors help keep you in check. If your game starts slipping, errors will show up in your performance.

Believe it or not, but some mistakes were meant to be made. The reason why is because the mistakes can reveal things that you may not have seen. For example, in the beginning of R&B singer Usher Raymond's career, he sung in a boy group that wasn't making the success that his mother felt they should have had. As a result, the group split up and went in different directions.

Usher was devastated and unsure of what to do. He decided to take a chance as a solo artist. Today, he is considered to be one of the most popular performers in the world. Now if he was still in that boy group, he may have never reached the success that he has today as a solo artist. What was viewed as a mistake in his childhood is now viewed as a blessing in his career. But it took that bad experience to help him receive his blessing. In other words, he had to take a chance.

Chances ~ Opportunity

When you believe in your potential, you'll realize that you may have to take chances to achieve the things that you want in life. Chances can be viewed in two different ways, as an opportunity or a risk. People that have faith in their ability and are passionate about their goals, view a chance as an opportunity.

People that doubt themselves and do not believe in their talent, view a chance as a risk. When you see stars and entertainers on TV, you see people that took chances as an opportunity. In order for them to be where they are they had to take chances.

For example, Sean "Diddy" Combs went to college at Howard University in 1987. He was known for his skills as a dancer in clubs and music videos. While on the set of music videos, he noticed the people that were behind the cameras. He saw the directors and music A&Rs who controlled what went on in the videos and in music. He wanted to learn more about what they did.

Combs decided to explore different opportunities to learn more about the music industry. The most notable record company closest to him was a company called Uptown Records. It took a four-hour train ride for him to get to Uptown Records from Howard University. That's right, four hours!

Sean was so eager to learn that he offered to do what most people never will; he asked to work for FREE. While other people his age were partying and having fun, Sean went to school and paid his dues volunteering at Uptown Records. For six months, he humbled his self by doing tasks that didn't have anything to do with music. Sean had to wash cars, make coffee, and run errands for people at Uptown Records.

Diddy "did" whatever he was asked. This type of work showed that he was passionate, reliable, persistent, and humble. When an A&R position became available, Sean was given the opportunity to earn it. He earned his place and achieved the goal that he set forth.

Today, Sean "Diddy" Combs is one of the most well-known people in entertainment. But none of his success would have ever taken place, if he hadn't believed in himself and taken a chance. So when a chance comes to you in life, you have two ways to look at it. You can see it as an opportunity or you can see it as a risk. I encourage you to take advantage of your chances and fulfill your potential.

Struggle comes before Success

One of the problems that we have when it comes to achieving our goals and fulfilling our potential is patience. In society today, everyone wants what is called a "microwave life." This means that we want everything in a hurry. We expect to see success as soon as we strive for it.

Well, I can save you a lot of trouble by telling you right now that struggle comes before success. Don't think for a second that everything is going to be easy for you, especially when you're trying to achieve excellence. It's going to take hard work and patience for some of the things that you want in life.

Believe it or not, but the things that take longer for us to have are more precious to us than the things that we get with ease. The reason why is because when you have to work hard for something, you have more appreciation for it. For example, think about when you have to save your paychecks for a month so that you can buy a new cell phone. I'm pretty sure that you'll appreciate that cell phone a lot more than if someone just gave it to you. When you save up your money for a whole year just so that you can pay a down payment on a car, you're going to show a lot of respect for that car. The reason why you show more respect is because you know how hard you had to work to get it.

Go Get Yours

Melissa "Missy" Elliott is a person that came from nothing and made something because she was a believer. As an only child, Missy was raised in a vermin-infested shack in Virginia. Being raised in poverty was by far the biggest obstacle facing the young Missy. As a child, her own cousin raped her consistently for close to a year.

To make matters worse, Missy Elliott's father beat on her mother every day and was even forced out of the house naked. Most people raised in this type of situation lose all hope for a normal life. Missy sought much more than just a normal life.

A determined Melissa "Misdemeanor" Elliott believed in her talent and saw music as an escape to a better life. She soon became recognized for her songwriting ability. She formed an R&B group with neighborhood friends that gained the attention of R&B producer, DeVante Swing and ultimately a deal with Elektra Records in 1991.

Yet, success for Missy would not come easy. The group recorded an album that never got released and the 20-plus group members eventually parted ways. The breakup of the group could have been a sign for Missy to abandon her dream. Still, she continued to believe.

Missy and neighborhood friend Timothy "Timbaland" Mosley partnered together as a songwriting/ production team. They developed hits for 90's R&B groups SWV and 702, but struck platinum when they worked with the late Aaliyah in 1996 for her second album *One in a Million*. The success as a songwriter and producer could have been enough, but Missy believed she could also reach success as an artist. She began to appear on songs as a featured artist in hopes to one day release her own songs as a solo artist.

The strong belief in her talent as an artist ultimately rewarded her a label deal with Elektra Records. In 1997 she released her solo debut *Supa Dupa Fly* on her label, The Goldmind Inc. Missy's belief in becoming a top-selling artist became a reality with the purchase of her debut album from more than a million fans. The album went on to become certified platinum and Missy went on to become one of the most influential artists in hip-hop. Her success was achieved because she refused to accept where she came from and only believed in where she was going.

No one at Def Jam or Roc-A-Fella believed in 'Through the Wire'. So I shot a video using my own money.

--- Kanye West

Kanye West is another great example of a person who reached success due to his everlasting belief in himself. Born in Atlanta and raised in Chicago, Kanye was raised in the suburbs where education played a pivotal role in his upbringing. His mother was a college professor, which meant that college would not even be optional for the young Kanye.

Kanye maintained grades of A's and B's throughout high school and enrolled in Chicago State University. As a full-time student, he also began producing for local artists in Chicago. The passion for music ultimately led Kanye to pursue his love full-time. He dropped out of college to become a full-time music producer.

For two years, Kanye West delivered beats to up and coming local artists within Chicago. Believing in himself and his talent, Kanye chose to move to New York in hopes to work with a broader range of artists. In 1998 his reputation as a producer became solidified when he began working with mainstream acts Jermaine Dupri, Foxy Brown, Goodie Mob and Harlem World. His name became even more familiar in 2000 when he began working with industry powerhouse

Roc-a-Fella Records (later known as RocNation). His signature production sound and beat patterns became instantly in demand among artists.

Similar to Missy Elliott, Kanye was considered as one of the hottest producers before he chose to record his own material. It would have been easy to only focus on succeeding as a producer and hit maker. Yet, Kanye believed that he could be just as popular in the recording booth, as well as behind it. He began to push demo discs of his music to record labels in hopes to secure a deal as a solo artist. Sadly, many labels claimed that Kanye did not have the right image and could never generate a real fan base for his music.

Kanye continued to believe in his potential as an artist. He spent hours before and after recording sessions booked with other artists to record his own material. Even after a near fatal car crash following a late night studio session, Kanye continued to record.

With his mouth half-wired shut, West recorded the lyrics for his first single appropriately titled, *Through the Wire*. He spent his own money to record a video promoting the song. His investment and belief in his own sound paid off tremendously. The song, along with his debut album *College Dropout,* reached triple platinum in sales and Kanye went on to become one of the top selling artists of the 2000s.

What doesn't kill you makes you stronger (also the title of one of Kanye's most popular singles) is one of the most notable phrases ever said. When it comes to your goals, you have to be a believer no matter how drastic the measures may be. No matter what others say or think you must never stop believing in you. Kanye West is living proof of what can happen in your life when you never stop believing.

When you choose to stop settling and start believing you can definitely touch the sky.

Do YOU

Remember, in life no one else can live your life but you. In order to make the most out of life you must believe in yourself. There shouldn't be anyone in the world that believes in your potential more than you. If you believe in your talent, others will begin to recognize it.

You have to be the first person to believe in you. Once you believe, you'll begin to achieve. You're passion will become a reflection of your talent, making it a natural reaction for you to achieve excellence.

Once you begin to achieve, you will begin to interpret your vision to succeed. As you succeed in your goals, remember to reflect on the challenges you may have faced along the way. Reflecting on your past obstacles will help you appreciate your accomplishments even more because you understand what it took for you to achieve them.

****

Take Notes:

Always believe in yourself and your dreams. Remember that you were born for a purpose. That purpose was to achieve excellence.

- Never allow someone else to crush the goals you have set for yourself.
- Don't expect for success to come without struggle.
- No one should believe in you more than yourself.

Stay far from timid, only make moves when your hearts in it, and live the phrase sky's the limit.

> -- Christopher "Notorious B.I.G." Wallace

What do you hope to pursue in life? Why do you want to pursue this? Do you know of any family members, friends, or people that are doing what you hope to do someday? How did they get to where you hope to eventually end up?

Keep Your Focus

Keep working hard and you can get anything that you want. If God gave you the talent, you should go for it. But don't think it's going to be easy. It's hard!

------Aaliyah

How many friends do you know that have goals? One week, they talk about how much they want to work hard at one thing. Soon after the previous week, they talk about achieving a different goal. Another week later, they have a different goal. Pretty soon they have a different goal every week. These would be remarkable accomplishments if these people didn't forget to do the most important thing, ACCOMPLISH the goals!

Accomplish your goals, do not just keep making new ones! The problem with so many people is that they can't complete goals after they establish them. In other words, they can't focus.

Be Consistent

It is important that once you set a goal that you focus on achieving that goal. Don't be the type of person that sets goals and doesn't put forth the effort to achieve them. There are so many people in the world today that talk too much and don't do anything to back it up.

Even the people in our families talk and don't act. Have you ever been to a family reunion? Do you have that cousin or uncle that's always talking about his life and how he was going to do this or do that? (This person is also usually the one that makes a fool out of himself because they're drinking beer all day.) Everyone in the family knows that he didn't and he won't do anything that he's ever talked about doing.

You never want to be viewed like that cousin or uncle. Do your best to remain consistent with your goals. Consistency is important because once you quit on one goal; it'll become easier to quit another.

Here's an example of an Uncle Bud.

> **Uncle Bud**: Hey boy, watcha know good!

(What is a "watcha know")

> **You**: Hey Uncle Bud.

> **Uncle Bud**: Boy, when I was your age I coulda done anything I wanted to. I could've gone on to the NFL or NBA. I would've been too much for em.

Here's an example of Cousin Jerry.

> **Cousin Jerry**: What up their cuz?

> **You**: Hey cousin Jerry.

> **Cousin Jerry**: Boy, ya know I'm bout to get signed to a label. My album is almost done.

> **You**: Didn't you say you were already signed?

Keep Your Focus

Believe it or not, in every family there's an Uncle Bud and a cousin Jerry.

I will admit it is difficult to stay focused in life, especially as a teen-ager. There's so many distractions and challenges that we face as teen-agers each day. Peer pressure is a huge distraction for us. Our peers tempt us to use drugs, hate church, hate school, have sex, and waste our time doing nothing. Your peers force you to not care about your dreams or goals that you have in life.

For the record, peer pressure is nothing more than a politically correct excuse. Society came up with this term for people who allow other people to influence them to do wrong. Believe what you want, but no one should have enough power over you to make you do anything you don't want to do.

People who use peer pressure as an excuse are those who are afraid to stand on their own two feet. Imagine how much trouble could be prevented if people chose to think for themselves instead of allowing their actions to be controlled by "peer pressure." It's time for us to grow up young people.

Destroy your Distractions

A key quality of a focused person is the ability to eliminate distractions. People who are destined for greatness will never get there without first removing those things that can be considered as a distraction. A distraction should be defined as anything that may prevent your progress. Distractions eventually lead to delays, which eventually stop you from moving forward.

Everyone has someone or something in his or her life that could be considered as a distraction. The difference between those people and focused people is that people who are focused are able to control anything that may interfere with them reaching their potential. A focused person knows how to block out disturbance. A good example of this might be a tight-rope walker at a circus or a basketball player making clutch free throws during crunch time in a close game. Successful people know how to tune out distractions when their future is on the line.

Establish your Priorities

Another vital key of a focused person is someone who has his or her priorities in order. Establishing your priorities in life literally itemizes how you should spend your day. Your tasks and responsibilities should be arranged in the order of importance.

Balance your time and energy towards achieving the goals that are of most importance first. Having your priorities in check means that you have an agenda. People without an agenda are those who are not focused.

Imagine an award show or Sunday church service without an agenda. There would be no type of order or structure. It would be absolute chaos! That's the way your life works without an agenda; total chaos.

There is no way you can consider yourself to be focused without an agenda. Having your priorities established provides order to your life. Imagine if a teacher never came to class without an agenda. You would not know the correct information to review for your exams.

You establish your priorities by first identifying what is required of you. Whether school work, job duties, household chores, football practice, dance rehearsal, etc. Ask yourself what are the consequences if you do not meet the requirements of each task required of you? How will each consequence affect your goals? You want to establish your priorities based on this criterion. This determines how and what you should focus on.

Establishing priorities and having an agenda not only allows you to focus, but it also gives each day a purpose. Waking up at 12pm on Saturday and playing video games all day is not a purpose-filled life. Focused people know how to structure their day in a way that allows them to be most effective. Rather than waste time, a person who has their priorities in order strives to make the most of it.

Down time is not the name of the game.

--- Usher Raymond

Monitor your Down Time

Anyone who desires to be successful in life should be encouraged to make the most out of each and every day. You must maximize each minute of every hour and each hour of every day. In this world there is no such thing as "free time." Each and everyday of your life you "spend time."

You spend time at school or at work. Parents spend time with their kids. Kids spend time with their friends. Young people must understand that the time you spend can and will never be returned. Therefore time should not be wasted.

When you work hard and complete your tasks you have then earned what should be considered as down time. Down time should be considered as earned. You earn down time once you have met your priorities and accomplished those things required of you. Completing your class projects, homework or duties within your household leads to potential down time. However, even down time should be managed responsibly.

Once you complete those things required of you why not take initiative to see what more you can do to succeed? Research how to achieve more of your goals or begin to work towards those goals. The most successful people within the industry will tell you that down time is not an option. They will tell you that any available minute is spent towards making things happen.

If you plan on making it as a singer or music producer every minute of down time can be spent towards making your dream a reality. Whether it's taking singing lessons, recording your sound, making connections with other artists or promoting your talent, there is always something else you can do to achieve that ultimate goal.

Russell Simmons created what would become a multi-million dollar music label named Def Jam right out of his college dorm room. The computer program (Microsoft) that would later make him one of the wealthiest human beings of all-time was developed by Bill Gates during his first two years in college. These guys were not wasting time chasing girls and $200 sneakers. They used their down time to create their own businesses. They saw down time as "grind time."

In order to achieve maximum results, you must maximize your down time and get on your grind. You have to put down the video game controller or TV remote and *go get yours*. Your down time should be converted into grind time.

Managing your down time is one of the utmost principles in staying focused. The easiest ways to control how you spend your down time can be found from reviewing your *plan* and establishing priorities within your weekly schedule. There should not be one day in the week that you don't know what you should be doing. You should have an agenda and be encouraged to stick to it.

Having a Role Model

One of the best ways to keep your focus is when you have a role model or someone to observe who remains focused. A **role model** is someone that sets a good example for others to follow. An example of a role model for young people could be Lebron James. Lebron grew up in a poor neighborhood without a father. The people in his neighborhood either sold or used drugs while he went to school.

Instead of using his situation as an excuse for him to fail, Lebron focused on his dream. When his teachers told him to pick a more realistic dream, he refused. His hard work and success as a basketball star proves that you can achieve your dream. But what's most important is that throughout his struggle in a difficult situation, Lebron remained focused.

Remember that a role model does not have to be someone who is famous or well-known. Anyone that sets a good example for others and shows others the difference between right and wrong is a role model. A role model could be your coach at school, teacher, pastor, parent, or friend. Take a second to think. Do you have a friend that always seems focused and accomplishes their goals? Do you set a good example for others?

Make a run while you're YOUNG

Many may not realize it, but a person's opportunity to achieve excellence is usually greatest when younger. The older you get, the more baggage you begin to pick up along the way. Love and responsibility begin to creep their way into the picture. Girlfriends become young wives and/or *baby mamas*. Your time eventually becomes in demand. Your focus begins to get cluttered.

In order to take a good shot at success you must remain

focused at an early age. Your mind needs to be affixed to making it, not making trouble. The easier you lose focus, the easier it is to become distracted. The harder you focus, the easier it is to destroy any distractions.

Young Man Making Moves

Nick Cannon is probably one of few people in the history of entertainment to have made a successful run in movies and television. What's more impressive is that he has succeeded in both categories, whether in front or behind the scenes. What's most impressive is that he achieved both at a young age. Nick's success was attained because he was always focused. While some chose to waste time getting into things that were destructive, a young Nick was on the move doing whatever it took to accomplish his goals.

Nick grew up with his mom in San Diego, CA. With limited income, the two were no exceptions to the ups and downs that so many face today. A teenage Nick chose to remain positive by using entertainment as his source of strength. He didn't look for entertainment, but instead chose to entertain. He realized that he could make others happy through his talent. Nick decided to use his talent to take him as far as it would go. Even if it meant commuting two hours back and forth to Los Angeles.

Nick Cannon remained on the go whenever an opportunity to showcase his talent in Los Angeles was available. He performed stand-up comedy at comedy clubs within Los Angeles. His appeal managed to land a spot on the Nickelodeon TV show "All That" in 1998.

Four years later he was awarded his own self-titled, "The Nick Cannon Show." The rest is history. He went on to become involved in more television shows, movies, music, fashion, radio and more. Nick's focus on his talent to entertain allowed him to succeed in multiple outlets. He was able to apply that focus to every opportunity and become successful.

Young people who are focused usually possess a drive that can easily be noticed. A person's drive stands out to others like a rose that grows through the cracks of concrete. The smell of a person's drive is as strong as the smell of barbecue at a black family reunion. The drive of a focused person is without a doubt an undeniable force. Your drive is stored inside of you, but it can only develop when you are focused.

Prepare to Sacrifice

One of the biggest problems for young people when staying focused is their inability to sacrifice. If you value your goals and dreams, please believe that you will have to make some sacrifices along the way. Most young people grow up with what is called a "sense of entitlement." So many of us believe that we are entitled to have everything we want handed to us.

As babies, we are born with everyone giving us everything we want to keep us happy. At some point, the luxury of having everything we want given to us should come to an end. The kids who continue to get a silver spoon are usually the ones who end up having the most problems during their transition into adulthood.

You cannot expect to achieve excellence if you are not willing to do whatever it takes. Think about it. If you want to be the best basketball player on the team, be prepared to practice more than everyone else. Be prepared to spend more time learning the plays. If it takes you all day and night to learn a new drill, make the sacrifice. But if you think that you'll wake up and dominate every game of the season without putting in some overtime on the practice court, you'd better go back to sleep.

> **Coach**: Hey I need you to stay after practice and run that play we just went over.
>
> **Player**: Aah, come on coach! I gotta do what?

This type of attitude is in no shape or form the attitude of a champ. If you want to be the best, show people that you can do what is necessary to become the best. This same concept of sacrifice must be applied to achieve any goal or dream. If you want to be an entertainer, you will have to dedicate your time to perfecting your skills. Sometimes it'll be fun, sometimes it won't. But you will have to be willing to put in lots of work and commitment.

A lot of times we see rappers, athletes, and entertainers on TV and we're in "awe" by their success. We watch them on TV and we want to experience life the way that they do. We begin to assume that if they can do it, then so can we. Some would even say that they got lucky to make it where they are. But don't believe any of that.

Successful people had to work HARD to get where they are today. They made sacrifices in their life that others could never imagine. These people knew what they wanted to be in life and they worked hard to get there. What's most notable is that they didn't let anything or anyone stop them on their mission to achieve greatness. Regardless of whether others doubted their future or abilities, these people maintained their will to succeed.

Maintain your Will to Succeed

For example, Allen Iverson grew up in poverty. As a kid, he was surrounded by people who doubted his size and ability to become a professional athlete. Instead of listening to them, he went on to become the player of the year in basketball and football in the state of Virginia as a junior at Bethel High School. Colleges from all over the country wanted him at their school.

At the end of his junior season, Allen Iverson and some friends were put in jail and expelled from school. Allegedly, they were accused of fighting with a group of white students at a bowling alley. Not only did he not play his senior year, but he had to go to a secondary high school just to receive his diploma.

All the colleges that wanted Allen Iverson the year before wanted nothing to do with him after he was expelled from school. This could have been a reason for anyone else to lose focus on his or her dream. Fortunately, Coach John Thompson believed in Allen Iverson's potential. Allen was fortunate enough for a chance to prove his talent and ability at Georgetown University, after so many others refused. He took that chance and kept his focus on his ultimate goal.

Allen Iverson worked hard during his two years at Georgetown and showed others his desire to be the best. He proved that beyond his obstacles in the past, he had what it took to be a professional basketball player. He proved it in front of the world when he was selected 1st overall by the Philadelphia 76ers in the 1996 NBA draft.

In 2001, Allen Iverson was voted the Most Valuable Player in the NBA. His achievement is a living testament to how far one can go when focused. What he went through should help you remember that in life you must remain focused, "no matter what."

The Power of Persistence

Another skill that is important when it comes to remaining

focused is *persistence*. We sometimes don't recognize persistence as a skill, although success can be measured from it. People underestimate its power, but you'd be surprised how far persistence can get you in life. It shows that you not only have passion, but it also shows that you're not afraid to be rejected in life.

The skill of persistence is what separates people that are successful from everyday "blue collar" workers. If you're persistent, it shows that regardless of what anyone else thinks, you're confident in yourself and your goals. Persistence is important because it proves your strength and will to succeed.

In the early 1990s, two 10th grade students joined together to form a rap group that would later on become the most successful rap duo in history. Their journey started when they met at Tri Cities High School in Atlanta, GA. Realizing their potential, they began performing for others to show how good they were. They performed anywhere someone would see them, even *gas stations*.

Soon the two students decided that they needed a name. After looking through a dictionary to find the best name to describe them, they came across the word *Outkast*. Eventually, they were able to perform before LaFace Records co-President, L.A. Reid. Although they were talented and filled with potential, L.A. Reid refused to offer them a deal.

This would have been an easy opportunity for Outkast to lose focus on their goal. The bad news left the group confused and discouraged for a brief period of time. Yet, there was one thing that kept them from quitting, *persistence*. Their persistence kept them from giving up on their dream. They practiced and worked even harder to perfect their craft.

From their lyrics to stage presence, these two guys molded themselves into the best performers they could be.

When Outkast got their 2nd chance to perform for L.A. Reid, they blew him away. They proved to him that they had what it takes to be stars in the industry. Mr. Reid couldn't have agreed more. He signed them that same day. Obviously, his decision was great for both LaFace and Outkast.

Today, Outkast is considered the most successful rap group *ever*. Their albums have sold more than any other group in the history of hip-hop. None of this would have been possible if they hadn't been persistent and focused. Before they sold albums, Outkast learned that they must first sell themselves.

One thing that can help you stay focused in life is to remember that there were others who came before you. A lot of us don't realize the sacrifices that others made in order for us to even have opportunity. The people that came before us didn't have half the opportunities that we have available to us now.

Today's generation has more than we even realize. Let's do the best that we can to not take these opportunities for granted. Better yet, we must make sure that we don't take for granted the sacrifices that people made for us to even have a chance.

Pay Homage by Staying Focused

Those that came before us played an important role in where we are today and the privileges that we have. We must learn to respect the struggle that they went through. They demonstrated, protested and marched so that we could have justice. They had to fight for our future.

There is no reason why we cannot achieve what we hope

to be. We must remember to stay focused as we go along in our journey. In a way, you could say that we must pay homage to those who came before us.

Homage is defined as showing or "paying" respect to someone by honoring them. There are plenty of ways that you can pay homage in your day-to-day life. When you show respect to your parents or anyone who's made a difference in your life, you're paying homage. When you go to school and work hard in your classes, you're paying homage. When you set a goal and focus on achieving that goal, you're paying homage. You pay homage when you do your best to make the most of yourself.

So when you feel like giving up or lose focus at something, you must remember the people you are letting down other than yourself. You're letting down the people before you who sacrificed so that you could have a chance. It is your responsibility to strive for excellence. The only person that can prevent you from achieving it is YOU.

You know you're focused when you:

1. Don't give in to the temptations of society (drugs, peer pressure, etc.)
2. Don't allow haters to disrupt your achievements
3. Have established a set of priorities
4. Stick to your agenda
5. Finish the things that you start

Those who are not focused should ask themselves:

1. How do you manage your down time?
2. What would you consider to be distractions that may prevent you from doing your best every day?

Keep Your Focus

3. Can you think of anyone who may distract you concentrating?

....

Take Notes:

Staying focused is one of the biggest obstacles in our road to success. We usually let others distract us such as friends, haters and family. Remember that no one in the industry got where they are today from letting others distract them. If you want to make it to the top, you have to keep your eyes on the prize.

Success for me isn't a destination it's a journey. Everybody's working to get to the top, but where is the top? It's all about working harder and getting better and moving up and up.

--- Rihanna

No Excuses

He that is good for making excuses is seldom good for anything else.

---Benjamin Franklin

If there is one lesson that you must learn immediately, you must learn that life is not fair. Life will never be fair for as long as you are living in this world. Things will never be fair for the remainder of your natural life. The quicker you understand this lesson, the quicker you can make progress and move toward success.

People who continue to think that life should be fair will find that their life will become a lot tougher than it should be. Instead of overcoming the unfairness in life, certain people choose to use what they think is unfair as excuses.

An excuse is probably the easiest thing that you can create in this world. It is also probably the most useless thing that you can create in this world. What is worse is that excuses are like potato chips. You can never make just one. The moment you start making an excuse you just open the door to make many more. You eventually become full of excuses. In short, you eventually become full of s(%)it.

No Age Limit to Succeed

One of the most common excuses for young people is that we are too young to strive for greatness. The myth is that there is a minimum legal age to reach for success. Many choose to believe that you are supposed to wait until you get into your late 20s or 30s before you can accomplish big things. Young people should be encouraged to go after goals as early as they can set them.

Great basketball players are great because they usually start playing at an early age. Multi-millionaires usually become rich because they started earning money at an early age. If you plan to be a millionaire, wouldn't it be smart if you start planning to make money at an early age?

The Internet moneymakers who invented Google, Youtube, MySpace and Facebook were all at the age of 25 and younger when their business ventures began to earn millions of dollars. Computer programmer Shawn Fanning was fresh out of high school when he launched and earned millions from the first popular file-sharing program, Napster.

Michael Dell, founder of computer brand Dell Inc., was destined for success from day one. Money that he earned as a teen from summer jobs was invested rather than wasted. He invested his hard earned money in stocks, not sneakers. In college, he developed an interest in computers. His interest led him to run a computer business directly out of his dorm room! In 1992 at the age of 27, Michael became the youngest CEO to have a company ranked in Fortune magazine's top 500 corporations.

You are never too young to decide that you are going to get off your butt and handle your business. A young man will never reach prominence if he always chooses to live off of excuses. Multi-billionaire Bill Gates was barely old enough to buy beer at a gas station when he decided to create his software company, Microsoft. Entertainer Eddie Murphy was barely in high school when he began to book gigs on stage at comedy clubs. To use the excuse that you are too young to strive for any goal is as weak as water.

How far do you think that minorities would have gone if we chose to always make excuses for ourselves? Chances are we would still be called "colored" and would sit at the back of the bus. Imagine how terrible young people would have it today if the late Dr. Martin Luther King Jr. had chose to sit on the porch, drink sweet tea all day and make excuses about why we can't do better for ourselves. Where would we be if other prominent people before us chose to sit back, relax and eat Funyuns' all day?

No Deposit No Return

Young people must realize that we can only expect to receive back what we deposit into our future. You cannot expect to receive the same results in a class when others are working hard and you're hardly working. Then you complain because you don't have the same opportunity as those who worked hard for what they have. Afterwards you find excuses and complain that life isn't fair.

Of course life isn't fair. Is it fair for you to expect to receive the same privileges as someone else who is working diligently every day? Is it fair for you to receive the same benefits as a person who sacrifices their spare time and puts forth maximum effort each day?

An excuse is usually made when a person fails to accept responsibility for actions or bad choices made. Everyone in this world has an opportunity to make an excuse each and every day of his or her life. The people who succeed in this world are those who refuse to make excuses. Losers are those who use excuses. Yet, I can guarantee that for every excuse there is also a solution.

In our lifetime, we are expected make mistakes. No one on this earth should expect to be perfect. One of the worst things you can do is to make excuses to cover up your error. If things are not going how you want them to go, be a man and own up to it. Boys make excuses. Men take action. Boys look to always blame others. Men accept responsibility. Boys wait until things happen. Men make things HAPPEN.

Excuses only excuse you from achieving progress. An excuse only admits to others that you are not on your game. Excuses say that you lack preparation and have no initiative. An excuse means that you cannot stand on your own feet and accept responsibility when things are not the way you want them to be. Excuses say that you are too lazy to find solutions to your problems.

The most prominent people usually came from harsh conditions as children. They didn't make any excuses. Why should you? They didn't let forks in the road stop their journey to success. Why should you? Nothing in this world can stop a person as long as they have a will to make it. Use each day to make strides to the top, rather than an earful of excuses.

Raised to Win

Out of all the people on this earth, I think that NBA legend Isiah Thomas could have made the most excuses for why success should have not happened in his life. Raised in a poor family as the youngest of nine children, Isiah probably never saw a new shirt or pair of shoes until he went away to college at Indiana University. Most parents complain when they have two or three kids to take care of. As a single mom, Ms. Mary Thomas had to take care of nine kids all by her lonesome. To make things worse, Isiah and his siblings were raised on the Westside of Chicago. In the 1970's, Chicago was infamous for the notorious street gangs that roamed the city. Yet, Isiah managed to avoid becoming another statistic to Chicago street life.

Isiah possessed a talent on the basketball court that provided an opportunity to attend a private high school in Westchester, IL. To leave everyday from the Westside of Chicago to Westchester is not exactly a quick drive around the block, but rather a journey. Instead of make excuses about the long distance, Isiah woke up at 5am each morning for a 90 minute commute by train to attend St. Joseph High School. His performance in high school led to a full scholarship at Indiana University, which ultimately opened the door to the NBA.

Many of us would have allowed excuses to stand in the way of the opportunities that awaited Isiah. In life we must learn that wherever there is a will, there is always a way. Isiah Thomas is an example of just how far you can go when you choose to not make excuses.

I guarantee that every successful person on earth can name one thing that should have prevented his progress. What counts is when you choose not to be stopped. No matter how many bricks are thrown in your path, you still have to keep walking. You still have to keep your head up. You still must keep looking ahead and not focus on where you are, but where you are going. No "noun" should be able to stop you. In other words, no person, place or thing should hold you back.

Meet Tyler Perry

Another good example of someone who refused to make excuses for himself is none other than media mogul, Tyler Perry. Born Emmitt Perry Jr, Tyler was raised in an abusive household. He was abused physically, mentally and even sexually. These harsh conditions would have been the perfect reason for anyone else to turn to a life of crime or drug addiction. Yet, Perry continued to strive.

As difficult as it may have been, Tyler Perry did not give up on what he could become one day. He used writing as a method to release his pain from the suffering he endured. He eventually discovered his God given talent as a writer and used it as a stairway to success.

Tyler Perry decided to first use his writing to release a play at a community center. With limited resources, Perry chose not to make any excuses. The 22-year old shelled out his life savings and invested in his production. Sadly, the movie did not provide positive feedback.

People dubbed his first production as a failure. Yet, people fail to realize that you only fail when you give up on yourself. Others may have seen this setback as an excuse to give up on his goal and waive a white flag. Instead, Perry spent the next decade perfecting his craft and developing productions for audiences across the country. In 2009, Perry was ranked by *Forbes* magazine as the sixth highest-paid man in Hollywood. As of July 2009, Perry's films had grossed nearly $400 million worldwide.

None of these people that have been mentioned would be where they are today had they chose to become victims of their circumstances. They would have never made it to the top if they used their negative experiences as excuses. No matter how hard you may think you have it in your life, you always have the option to succeed. What you have to decide is how bad do you want it? Then you have to decide just how hard you are willing to work for it?

No matter how broke, ugly, short, lanky, fat or disadvantaged that someone else considers you to be, you always have a shot at greatness. Every day that you wake up is a reason to go all out for excellence. Every day you breathe air is a reason not to have an excuse. Each day that you feel the wind blow on your neck is another chance that God has given to you. Why sit still and come up with excuses when you are given a new shot each day?

Launching BET

Another example of someone who chose not to make excuses and go for their dream is none other than Black Entertainment Television (BET) founder, Robert "Bob" Johnson. Raised in a family of ten children, Bob Johnson's upbringing was hardly any better than that of NBA great Isiah Thomas. Instead of focusing on how much he didn't have, Bob chose to focus on what he did have. He had an intelligent brain. As a youth, he realized that an education would be the only way to succeed. He worked hard in his schoolwork and earned an academic scholarship to Illinois University.

Bob Johnson's hard work led him to receive his Master's degree in public administration from Princeton University. After putting in years of work for PBS and the Washington Urban League, Johnson landed a position with the National Cable and Television Association. It was here where Johnson developed his dream and vision for his own cable network. It was a dream that for most would remain just a dream due to excuses for why it could never happen. Bob Johnson chose to find ways to make his dream a reality.

As a man who never came from money, Bob Johnson realized how expensive it would be to start a cable company. Rather than sit back and cry about the costs, Bob found investors and secured loans from banks. His vision eventually became a reality when BET took air for the first time in 1980. The reality of his vision ultimately came with long and even more expensive reasons that he could have used as excuses. Until 1989, Bob never received a profit from his dream.

It took nine years for Bob Johnson to pay back his loans and investors. So many of us would have seen this long period of struggle as an excuse to give up, but Bob Johnson hung on. Twelve years after the debut of his own network, Bob became a millionaire. Eventually, Robert "Bob" Johnson became the first African-American billionaire in the United States. If the 9th child in a poor family of 10 can make it, what's your excuse?

When you find yourself preparing to make an excuse for why you cannot do something, find a reason for why you can do it. For every possible excuse, destroy that excuse with a solution. Young people must learn to counter any excuse with a solution.

A definition of counter means a blow given while receiving or deflecting another blow. Like a boxer in a fight, you must counter any excuse that enters your mind. Whenever you begin to develop that excuse, your mind must immediately counter it with an answer.

Godfather of Urban Fashion

Carl "Karl Kani" Williams is a great example of what you can accomplish when you choose to counter excuses with solutions. Carl began designing clothes in Brooklyn at the age of 16, even without ever having studied how to design or tailor. What Carl did have was a creative mind to create stylish concepts and designs. He paid a tailor to help create custom outfits that no one had. Eventually, a buzz for his designs began to make way on the Brooklyn club scene and the young Carl was setting up orders for his clothing from his car. Carl's popularity, along with the death of a close friend, motivated him to take his talent for fashion as far as he could go.

In 1989, Carl chose to move to Los Angeles to pursue his dream as a fashion designer. The idea of a young, black man with his own hip-hop clothing line is very common today, but in the late 80's it was unthinkable. Who would imagine that a 21-year old could market a clothing line or even a business?

Carl asked a question to himself repeatedly. He asked the question "can I" so often that he chose to attach the question to his name. He replaced the "c" in his name with a "k" and changed the spelling of "can I" to "Kani." With the name "Karl Kani," he and a friend opened a clothing shop on Crenshaw Boulevard. Yet, tough times were ahead.

Karl's first year in business resulted in no profit and a robbery in his clothing shop. This is a setback that many would have used as an excuse, but the rough year did not stop his hustle. Karl got on his grind and moved to Hollywood. He and a friend sold catalogs of their clothing and placed ads in magazines. Still, Karl had little to show for his efforts. With no results and no profit, he had a universal excuse to quit on his dream. Rather than suffer into making excuses, Karl chose to counter with solutions.

What eventually boosted clothing orders was an idea to have a friend in New York hold up a sign of the Karl Kani logo during a taping of NBC's "Today Show." The brand began to develop attention even more when Karl chose to increase the pant size for jeans, dubbing the term "baggy jeans." Retailers opened the door to Karl's clothing and profits began to boom for his clothing line.

In 1996, Karl was labeled one of the 100 richest African-Americans and later invited to present his fashion line at the White House to President Bill Clinton in 1999. He is considered as the "Godfather of Urban Fashion" and "The Originator" of all hip-hop clothing. His success would have never been possible had he not countered excuses with ideas and solutions.

In life we must realize that ultimate rewards usually require overcoming ultimate challenges. One should never deny a challenge and expect to make progress. Challenges can be overcome through sacrifice, not excuses. As long as you have a will to achieve, you can always overcome any obstacle. From this chapter you should learn to never deny a challenge. This chapter should teach you to never allow your will to succeed be denied.

Airing Radio One

The potential for success can never be denied, no matter how tough the situation may be. A great example of this is Radio One, TV One and Interactive One founder, Catherine Hughes. She got her start in radio as the general manager of WHUR-FM radio station at Howard University in Washington, D.C.

Hughes eventually decided to create her own radio station. Her desire to start her own station was put to the test after being denied for a loan by 32 banks, giving her 32 excuses to call it quits. Her "never quit" attitude finally secured a loan and she created Radio One with the purchase of a destroyed AM radio station. Yet, Cathy's battle for success was far from over.

The effort to renovate the former AM radio station and broadcast her own station forced Catherine Hughes into immediate financial difficulty. Many people would have used such financial woes as the perfect excuses to end the dream, but Hughes chose to adjust and sacrifice. The single mother was eventually forced to raise her child and her dream at the radio station. She cooked meals on a hot plate and bathed in the office restroom. At the time she may have not had much money, but Hughes was filled with visions and ideas.

Catherine Hughes took that diminished AM station and transformed it into a successful 24-hour talk radio station. The success with one station went on to the ownership of more than 70 stations. Hughes ultimately became the first black woman to lead a publicly traded company. She reached the top because she chose to never give up on her dream. Her dream drove her to make history, rather than excuses. If a single-mother can successfully create and run a multi-million dollar empire, there's no excuse why you cannot achieve any goal you set.

The will to succeed can take you farther than your peers could ever imagine for you. Doubt only develops into potential excuses. Those excuses will keep your potential nailed to the ground. Keep it moving when doubt and excuses come towards you. Don't let either one keep you grounded. Look towards solutions that will keep you moving forward. The biggest solution always remains in you. Never let any excuse blind you from seeing that.

Take Notes:

Excuses will never help you move forward, but only backwards.

Excuses only excuse you from achieving progress.

Learn to counter an excuse with a solution.

The people who succeed in this world are those who refuse to make excuses.

No one is immune to the trials and tribulations of life.
--- Martin Lawrence

Think First

Have you ever heard your friends say, "*you know what I'm saying*," "*know what I'm talking bout*," "*ya heard me*," or "*ya understand?*" The trap that we fall into with using these phrases is that we can't stop using them. They become a habit that's too hard to break. Once we try to stop using them, we accidently do. Imagine being interviewed for a job. While you're answering a question, you accidently say, "*know what I'm talking bout?*"

> **Interviewer**: I've reviewed your resume and see that you are a great candidate for this position. Why do you think we should hire you?
>
> **Derek**: Well I feel that my experience in my previous employment makes me well-qualified for this position, "know what I'm talking bout?"

As a young minority, you have to be able to speak with intelligence. Society assumes that you don't have the ability to speak intelligently. They expect you to use slang because they think that it's the only way you know how to speak.

When you are in class, church, or in front of anyone that you respect, show them respect by speaking with intelligence. When I say intelligence, I don't mean to speak to them with arrogance. An arrogant person is someone that loves to let others know how great they are, even if nobody wants to know. They use complicated words that others don't understand. Believe it or not, but a lot of times arrogant people use words that they don't even understand.

Arrogance is not a positive attribute so do not develop it. Just speak to people in a way so that they recognize you have common sense. If you don't, people will automatically assume that you're a fool. That's something that you definitely don't want because then they'll never respect anything that you have to say.

Young people should try their best to develop the ability to speak intelligently. It's a shame when someone is unable to get a job because they don't know how to use proper English. What makes it so difficult for our generation is that we learn our language from so many places besides the classroom. We allow what we see on TV and in movies to teach us how to speak, walk, dress, and even THINK. Then, we pass on whatever we learn to our friends. Then, our friends pass on to us what they learn.

What we must realize is that TV is not real. People watch TV for entertainment, something that our culture seems to misunderstand. We get "caught up" in what we watch and sometimes act the way we see people on TV. That's why it's important that you don't spend so much time watching it. TV will confuse you if you watch it too much.

A lot of parents recognize how powerful TV is to us as young people. Some parents even try to limit the amount of TV that we watch. If you're sitting at home all day watching music videos, what can you possibly expect to learn? Other than learning the latest dances, slang and fashion, there isn't much that you can learn to help you in the "real" world. That's why it's crucial that you understand this while you're young. Imagine somebody 30 or 40 years old at home watching music videos all day, dancing in front of the TV hollering, *"what they do!"* That's a fool.

Catch the catch phrase

A lot of us have friends that love to say, *"ya know what I'm saying?"* Now nothing is wrong with that except for one problem. They say it too much! If someone has to say, *"ya know what I'm saying"* after every sentence, then there's a problem.

> **Dominic**: I was sittin down in class……. "ya know what I'm saying?"
>
> Then the teacher came in……. "ya know what I'm saying?"
>
> She told us to turn to page….. "ya know what I'm saying?"

Listen to how silly this sounds. It makes no sense for you to ask someone if they understand you. A lot of people think that it's okay or cool, but it's not. It's ignorant. If you're a good friend, help your friends break this cycle of ignorance. Unless someone lets them know how often they repeat that phrase, they don't know how critical it is.

Whenever someone asks, *"you know what I'm saying"*, *"know what I'm talking bout"*, or any other phrase, simply say NO. Think about it. When you say no, you'll encourage your friends to explain what they're saying rather than assume *ya understand?*

Another phrase that our culture has fallen in love with is *"you know how it is."* Whenever we're late for something that's important, we love to use the excuse *"you know how it is."* Why do we assume that others understand our negligence?

> **Aaron**: Yo Chris, what happened to you? We were supposed to start on our class project an hour ago. Why are you late?

Chris: Man I had to go take care of something dawg. Come on brother. *You know how it is.*

See how we use this phrase as a crutch to get over on others who depend on us? It's as if we expect people to understand our laziness. Instead of taking the time to be responsible, we assume that others will accept what we do. In other words, we take advantage of those who are kind to us. Once they confront us about our actions, we think that they're the ones with the problem. Think about how funny that sounds. But sometimes that's the way we act.

Destroy the "N" word

The phrase that we use the most is not a phrase at all, but only a word. It's the word that was once forbidden. That's right, you guessed it, THE "N" WORD. The one word that we definitely need to learn to control is the word "*nigga*." People don't realize how loose the use of this word has become.

Most of us use the "N" word when we talk to our friends or when we make conversation with others. But what we don't realize is that white people use this word just as much as we do! They call themselves and even their black friends *niggas*. Some African-Americans have started to accept it and become cool with it! This word has gotten so comfortable in the hip-hop culture that everyone uses it as if it's the only word in the world.

As minorities, we need to be careful with what we say and whom we say it around. You can't expect white people to stop using this word if you're constantly using it around them. When you say the "N" word around white people it just makes them want to use it too. The best thing that we can do as minorities is to stop using this word.

Find a way to speak to your friends without having to say "*nigga this*" and "*nigga that.*" Try to find a substitute like: *homie, black, fam, bro*, etc. Don't get it wrong, using the "N" word is ignorant! It's important that as young people we recognize it. We think it's funny to hear a person use it when joking on someone, but it's not funny at all when a white person says the "N" word. It's not funny or cool, and it NEVER should be.

Choices, Decisions and Consequences

One of the biggest regrets that you can have is to make decisions without considering the consequences in the future. Kids today are making terrible decisions that can harm them later in life. For example, on TV you see entertainers with gold and platinum grills in their mouth. Naturally kids see this and they too want to get platinum in their mouth. But what kids don't realize is that entertainers are selling their image to you.

Entertainers and rappers are trying to appeal their image to you so that you will go out and purchase their new CD or see them at a concert. They are getting paid! They're job is to appeal and entertain you. Kids today want to get gold and platinum in their mouth, but they need to understand the consequences of these actions. If you go out and get gold or platinum put permanently into your mouth, you may not be able to get a job.

Years ago, everyone wanted to get their ears pierced so that they could rock earrings. There's nothing wrong with that. The great thing about earrings is that they're removable. You can remove them if you need to.

Now when it comes to tattoos, just be careful. Make sure that whatever you decide to put on you is something that you can be proud of FOREVER, because it will be on you FOREVER. Don't just go walking into the tattoo shop and pick anything. Get something that's meaningful.

There is nothing wrong with getting a tattoo when there is a meaning behind it. Tattoos help you to never forget and to always remember. But the tattoos that people get on them today are just crazy. It's as if people just don't think first. Remember that you're getting a tattoo, not a haircut.

Tattoo artist: Hi, what can I do for you?

J-dog: What it do. Let me get a skeleton holding a 9mm in his hand. And on the bottom put "Thugged Out!"

Young brothers and sisters you need to think carefully about your choices. What's even worse is the location that some people put their tattoos at. It's hard to understand why someone would put a tattoo directly on his neck or face.

Not to say that you have to keep your tattoos covered, but you don't want to put them on a place that can NEVER be covered. Imagine meeting a girl's parents for the first time. You walk up to her father with "thug life" tattooed to your neck. You look crazy!

The way we represent ourselves is critical. You may not recognize it today, but it can be devastating in the long run. Young people should be aware that life is about choices, decisions and consequences. The choices you make today can come with drastic consequences tomorrow.

Young people should be advised to make choices with caution. You can live for today, but also plan for tomorrow. Ask yourself if the choice you're about to make will benefit or hurt you in your future. A few minutes of fame are not worth tarnishing opportunities that wait in the future.

Reality TV has probably the biggest source of people who can testify that bad choices today can become roadblocks for tomorrow.

Former Public Enemy rapper Flavor Flav had one of the highest rated shows on television, "Flavor of Love." The show was based on 15 women competing on national TV to be with Flavor Flav romantically. The show aired everything from fights, sexual encounters, spitting and almost any immorality that you can think of. Now I have nothing against a woman willing to give her all for the man she loves, but how can you love someone when he's slamming his tongue down every throat he sees! Not only that, but to have it all televised in front of millions of households! How can you expect someone to take you seriously in a job interview when they saw you competing to tongue wrestle with a guy on television?

The young and fresh generation should be encouraged to think about the choices that they make each and every day. Society already loves to expose all of our flaws and negatives. Why choose to aid them in the process of holding you back or tearing you down? Regardless of anyone else's opinion, you should do your best to make choices that will benefit you in the long run. Choosing to have a threesome on national TV may give you instant fame for a year, but how will it affect you in the long run?

For years networks have continued to make millions off of so many young people choosing to make fools of themselves. Television networks such as MTV, VH1 and even BET have cashed in on broadcasting the foolish antics of our young generation. Rather than challenge this negative behavior, society chooses to promote what we should consider as bad decision-making. Choosing to expose our flaws before the world may come with more cons than pros.

Before you decide to blast yourself on TV, ask yourself are you willing to pay that price?

Think Before You Speak

The thought process of our culture can be hilarious at times. Not just the way we think, but how our mind operates. We think that a person is LAME if they talk intelligently. In other words, you can only be cool unless you use slang. That's how most of us think. Why? Why is it that we think this way?

Usually if we notice someone with glasses on, we show him more respect because we assume he is intelligent. When it's time to take a test, everyone wants to study with Urkel. They recognize this person for their intellect, but they don't think of him as cool. The question that we need to ask ourselves is why do we feel like we can't be smart and cool? Our culture needs to understand that you can be both.

Usually when someone speaks proper and clearly, we want to put that person down because we think he is not "down." A lot of us cut off these types of people, when instead we should network with them. Networking is when people connect with one another to expand opportunity.

The ability to network is a skill that young minorities need to develop. The reason why is because people that could help you move up in life can't because you don't take the time to make friends with them. On the other hand, successful people are the exact opposite. Even though they may not like someone, they never cut them off. They know that in the long run that person may become successful and be able to help them in some way. This is called, SMART.

Young people need to understand how to "network" rather than do what we are known to do, HATE. Think

Think First

about it. If you see someone in class that speaks properly and looks presentable, don't you think that person might become successful? Why not become acquainted with that person and make a good connection. Nobody's saying that you have to be best friends. But don't burn your bridges with them by writing them off.

Now let us return to the original question. Why do we make fun of people that speak properly? Could it be we think they're LAME because they don't talk the way we hear people talk in the music we listen to or the videos and TV shows that we watch? In other words, we make fun of people that speak proper because they don't talk like we talk. We judge them and sometimes ask them, "why you trying to talk white" or "why you trying to be white?"

If you really think about it, accusing somebody of acting white is prejudice on our part as minorities. Could it be because we are judging our own people based on stereotypes the way others judge us? Most of us hate when white people judge us off our way of life and how we act. So why should we practice the same type of ignorance? It just doesn't make sense. Yet, it's something that we do and have continued to become comfortable doing.

Have you ever heard your friends tell someone, "Man, quit acting like you white!" Our culture needs to work together to stop this form of ignorant thinking. Think about it. If a white person begins to use slang, does that mean they're trying to act black? For example, if a white guy starts going around saying, "what they do," does that mean he's talking black. If you really think about it, society would say that if you're talking like you're black, that mean's you're talking foolish.

Society accuses "us" of speaking ignorant. In order for our culture to break this stereotype, we need to take a stance and show that we don't speak ignorance. We have to quit adding fuel to the fire society started. We must show others that we can communicate effectively, or in other words, INTELLIGENTLY.

College is a MUST

In order for us to speak with intelligence, sometimes we need to hear others speak intelligently. That's why it's so important that we make the attempt to go to college. We need to understand how critical a lack of education is to our culture. College helps to expose you to others that have goals and visions.

In college, people begin to develop a clearer picture of how the world operates. If you hang around your hometown too long, your view of the world becomes narrow. In other words, your hometown becomes your world. Your hometown may show you that you can't be cool and make good grades, but college will show you a different view. Your experience in college will help you understand that being smart is cool.

College allows you to mold your thinking and expand your mind. The experience of going to college is a help to young people in need of a change of perception. To speak with intelligence and apply good judgment is not as hard once you place yourself in an environment dedicated to higher learning. Your parents are responsible for laying down the foundation within you to achieve success. College is the place that allows you to build upon that foundation.

College allows you to step outside of your comfort zone and away from your normal surroundings. It gives you the opportunity to meet new people and learn information needed to become prepared for the real world. Attending college should not be thought of as an option to our young generation.

Take Notes:

Think first!

Do you use or hang with people that overuse the "N" word in public?

Do you fall into the trap of always making excuses for yourself?

Do you sag your pants in public?

The Way It Should Be

Have you ever liked someone so much that you got goose bumps whenever you saw them? When you got dressed for school, you wanted to make sure that you were fresh and clean. You wanted to make sure that when you approached that person that you were on point. That's the difference between today and back then.

Today, nobody wants to do the little things to impress someone they admire. Now guys walk up to girls and say, *"What it do girl, let me holla at you!"* Think about how silly that sounds, *"Let me holla at you!"*

People today do not show respect for others, nor do they show respect for themselves. This type of behavior could easily be stopped if it wasn't for one problem. Our young women have begun to accept and tolerate this type of behavior. Rather than date someone that shows class and treats them with respect, young women today are fascinated by thugs.

Let's take a minute to comprehend. Just to make sure that you're following along, let's break down some terms.

Classy – someone that shows respect for himself or herself; well kept; clean in appearance.

Thug – someone who has no class, nor respect for himself or herself; grungy looking; dirty

Back in the day, a girl would not even talk to a guy unless

The Way It Should Be

he was well groomed and polite. Today, guys walk around in dirty, white T-shirts with their underwear showing above their jeans. These guys don't even comb or brush their hair. What's even worse is their breath can smell like hot garbage, but some girls will stand right with these guys and hold a conversation. It's amazing how the times have changed.

Young men today should know when you see a lady around, do not yell, "Hey shawty!" Impress her by showing that you have class. She'll probably show you more respect because you approached her in a respectful manner.

As for girls, you don't have to lower your standards to be approachable for young men. Keep your morals and standards as you wish. If a young man can't respect your values, don't mess with him. Your values make you who you are. Make people respect you for that.

Young women must also remember to give some of these young men a chance before they dismiss them. Although there are a lot of young knuckleheads out here, there are a few gentlemen left. At least give these gentlemen the chance to show they have class. But remember, if he presents himself as a fool, GET AWAY and STAY AWAY.

R-E-S-P-E-C-T

Let's talk some more about this thing we call respect. Respect is one of the most important values in life. No amount of money can buy someone respect; yet respect is similar to money. Like money, respect is something that is earned.

Never respect someone that does not respect you. That doesn't mean that you should disrespect that person, just don't respect them. You can be the bigger person in the situation by tending to your own business, or as they say KEEP IT MOVING.

Rules of Respect:
- When you speak to someone, look that person in the eye. Looking a person in their eyes tends to make a person show more respect to you.
- Never respect someone that does not respect you.

During our development we all desire acceptance. One of the worst things you can do is to spend all of your energy trying to get everyone to accept you. People that do this only lead themselves into an identity crisis or become "fake." Fake people are those who allow others to define who they are. You have to define and first accept yourself.

When you accept yourself, others may begin to accept you. There is no guarantee everyone will like you, but they should have no reason to disrespect you. Choosing to please everyone only gives people the power to raise and define you.

The moment you define who you are you can begin to define where you are going. No one should completely change who they are. Yet, you can always redefine who you are.

So many young people end up making poor decisions because they want to gain respect. Many commit acts of crime or violence because they feel as though they have something to prove. In life we should never waste time seeking to gain another person's approval. Fighting to gain the respect of your peers is a battle that is not worth fighting. It is only when you are disrespected that you have a legit reason to stand tall.

Swag without Sag

Back in the day, the media would portray our culture as

The Way It Should Be

foolish. They would describe us as a group of ignorant people. For years we preached and demonstrated against these stereotypes. We made those who misunderstood us recognize that our culture was not foolish, but rather a form of art. We let society know that we expressed ourselves through our music, dance and fashion. There were people in the game who fought hard to make mainstream media understand and accept our way of life.

Today, it is as if we have lost our purpose. Our style of fashion and our music have become impossible to explain to society. A lot of us can't even explain it to ourselves.

Nobody in their right mind can explain why someone "sags" his pants. You can get the best lawyers in America. It's a guarantee that none of them will be able to justify why our culture "sags."

You got teens and young adults throughout the country fastening their pants *below* their butt. They don't even need zippers in their pants. When they have to use the bathroom, they just lift their shirt up. Now it's not as bad while you're young, but imagine a 30-year old man still *"sagging"* his pants. What type of sense does this make?

How can you call yourself a grown man walking around with your pants hanging off your butt? That's not *fashionable*. That's not a man. That's a clown!

Our culture needs to make an effort to break this form of foolishness. In prison, people would sag their pants to let other inmates know they were gay. Back then it was viewed as a sign of homosexuality, something that nobody wants to be accused of today.

Nobody's saying that you have to wear your pants like you're *Steve Urkel*. Just don't take it to the extreme. If your butt crack is exposed when you walk down the street, THAT'S EXTREME! Then when your parents or teachers question you about it, you want to get mad. Don't get mad, get *smart*. Wear your pants the way that they were designed for you to wear them, ON YOUR WAIST.

When you are unable to walk properly, chances are it is time to re-consider your pant size. What shall profit a man whose butt is always exposed to the world? Bring your pants up off your ass and pull up some form of dignity. Pick up a belt and grab some respect for yourself. How can anyone expect for people to show you respect when all you can show for yourself is the color of your underwear?

Keep Your Cool

Another big problem for us as minorities is that we make things a lot more difficult than they have to be. Either we talk too much or we act too crazy when it's unnecessary. At school, students decide to talk to each other while the teacher is trying to teach the class. When the teacher asks them to be quiet, someone just has to talk back, when all you have to do is just be quiet.

> **Ms. Jones**: Keyshawn please be quiet. Your interruptions are preventing your classmates from learning.
>
> **Keyshawn**: Why I got to be quiet? I ain't the only one talking!
>
> **Ms. Jones**: Fair enough. Take yourself down to the dean's office.
>
> **Keyshawn**: But……but…….
>
> **Ms. Jones**: I don't wanna hear it. I'm sure the dean and your parents can help you be quiet.

Why get yourself in trouble and make your parents get on you? That's the problem in society today. We just can't do as we're told or we feel like we have to show out. When you behave like this, the only thing that you're doing is making life difficult for yourself in the future.

Stop Shouting

Something else that we also need to do besides listen is to stop YELLING. It's funny how we talk loud when it's not necessary. We need to stop yelling all the time because it's degrading to our culture. It makes us look as if it's the only way we know how to communicate with one another. In other words, it shows a lack of home training. Better yet, it shows ignorance.

People see our actions and think we do not know how to behave properly, as if we are not civilized. We'll go to the movies, class, even the library, and yell to each other like we're at a football game. It's as if sometimes we just don't know how to be quiet when it's necessary. Then when someone politely asks us to quiet down, we take offense to it. We get loud and say, "*who you telling to be quiet,*" or "*you ain't my mama!*"

(BJ and Terry are talking in the library.)

BJ: YO TERRY, WHAT UP WITH SOME NFL MADDEN LATER ON.

Terry: YEAH, WE CAN GET DOWN ON IT.

(Mike, a classmate, is trying to study for a test)

Mike: Aye fellas, y'all mind keeping it down.

BJ: Man, what! Who you telling to be quiet?

Sometimes we fail to think about the situation. We're making all this noise and disrupting others and just *flat out in the wrong*, but we get angry and think that someone else is wrong for addressing our actions. If you ever encounter a situation like this, think first about the situation. Don't just go off on the person. Recognize your actions and check yourself.

Be on Time

Another thing that we must overcome as a culture is our preparation and promptness. As young people, it is important that we learn how to be on time. It's important to be on time, especially if you've told someone in advance that you will be on time. You want people to have respect for what you say and for your actions.

People that have a habit of coming to class late will eventually grow up to go to work late. That's why it's important that you destroy this habit at an early age. Once you start showing up late to one thing, you'll make it a habit to show up late for everything.

Believe it or not, a habit is just as addictive as a drug, maybe even more! That's why you need to make sure that the habits you do have are positive, rather than negative. So in case you haven't recognized it, being late is a negative habit.

When you arrive on time you show your desire to get ahead. It's important that you show a desire to achieve excellence. If you want to be treated with excellence, you have to show that you have a hunger for it.

Many times we joke others because they are on time and prepared. We make fun of them and call them "suck-ups." Instead of calling them suck-ups, we need to call them "examples." They should be called examples because they're constantly setting a positive example for others. They show us the way that excellence is achieved: through dedication, preparation and promptness.

Spend Wisely

Now if only someone could show us how to handle our money with excellence. When it comes to money, some would say that it makes the world go round. No matter what you want in life, money is involved in some sort of way.

Reports show that *African-Americans* spend more money than any other race in the world. Now if we spend the most money and money makes the world go round, then what does that say? It says that *African-Americans* make the world go round, LOUD and CLEAR.

Unfortunately, a lot of us do not understand the impact that our money has in the world. The people that do understand are the people that collect the money we spend. That's right, I'm talking about CORPORATE AMERICA.

We give corporate America a reason to make even more money off of us from the habits that we have. The more money we spend on liquor, the more $$$ they earn. The more we spend on rims, the more $$$ they put in their pockets.

Some of the companies that we make rich do not even appreciate our business. For example, rappers and entertainers love to buy bottles of *Christal* and brag about it in their songs. But the company behind *Christal* laughs at us behind our back, while they collect and count our money. They consider our demand for their product as "unwelcomed attention." In other words, they aren't for us.

A lot of people may not remember this, but in the

90s, *Tommy Hilfiger* was one of the most popular brands of clothing in the country. Parents used to spend all their money to buy their kids *Tommy* so that they could have their kids looking good for school. Eventually, *Tommy* became the most popular brand in the country because of the business that "we" brought their company.

All of a sudden, Tommy Hilfiger (the man) let everyone know how he felt about our business. He described our business as "not wanted." The funny part is that we were still buying his clothes and making him rich, after he told us that he didn't want our money. This is called bad spending.

Most Important Numbers

The biggest consequence of bad spending is that it gets worse as we get older. We start ruining something that will affect us for the rest of our lives. In case you don't know, I'm talking about "credit." Your *credit history* is as vital as a jail record.

There are two sets of numbers that affect your whole life, your social security number and your credit score. Your credit score can determine whether you can get a house, car and even a job. What's sad is that a lot of mistakes that affect credit are made at a young age.

The day you turn 18, credit card companies are breaking their backs to get you to accept their credit cards. It's even worse when you get to college. Companies try to offer credit cards to you as if they're giving you free money.

Some colleges even allow representatives from credit card companies to advertise and offer credit card applications *on campus*. They'll even offer free pizza to you, like they're doing you a favor. Imagine that. You end up spending money that you don't even have and pay more in interest because you accepted *free pizza for a credit card*. Sounds crazy, don't you agree?

The Way It Should Be

Learn to Invest

What our people must learn to do is not spend, but invest. When you invest in something, you're buying something that will appreciate in value. When something appreciates, its worth raises in value. A house, artwork and real estate are things that appreciate in value. Cars, rims, clothes and electronics are things that don't appreciate in value. Instead they begin to lose worth the moment you buy them.

Successful people understand the concept of investing before spending very well. They seek to put money towards things that will return money and profit. That's why they own nice homes, rather than nice clothes or a fancy car. While we're parking a tricked out Cadillac Escalade in the parking lot of our apartment, successful people are parking their classy Volvo into the garage of their mansion.

Sex

Then sooner or later, there is that one issue that we are going to deal with for the rest of our lives. You know what I'm talking about. There is one subject that everyone thinks about, but doesn't want to talk about. I'm talking about SEX.

Sex is and will always be a touchy subject. No matter how many people you talk to about sex, everyone will have a different view or opinion. That's why it's important that you get the facts. That way you can develop an opinion of your own about the subject.

So to help you develop your own opinion, let's hear a fact from the Bible. The Bible states that *sex was created so that a married man and woman could physically express their love for each other*. Notice how it says, "a married man and woman." In today's society, this fact has almost become extinct.

People have sex now just to prove that they are capable of doing it. Sex has become some type of sick contest. Think about it. How many times have you heard someone say, "how many girls have you *knocked off*?"

It is a shame that we do not appreciate the honor of a relationship or sharing love with someone that you have married. Yeah, it sounds corny, maybe even green. But sex was meant for expressing your love for someone. As young people, we don't want to hear this when others are always preaching it to us. The only time we're willing to listen is when we see the consequences of having sex before marriage. Like when your girl calls you one day and says the two most *frightening* words a young man can hear, "*I'm pregnant.*"

What we fail to understand is that people that are married are able to deal with the consequences and responsibilities of sex. You want to know why? The reason is because they planned for it. I'm pretty sure that two people that don't love each other are NOT expecting to have a child, especially two teen-agers.

Today, some teens are confused. They have unprotected sex, hoping to get someone pregnant so that they can have a child. They think that bringing a child into the world is cool, like it's a sign of RESPECT. Think about how silly this sounds. Better yet, think about how ignorant it sounds. How can you make such a silly decision that can jeopardize your life and your future? Young America, PLEASE WAKE UP!

....

You have reached the conclusion of this book. I encourage you to not allow this book to get too far away from you. Read it. Make sure that you understand what you've read. If you didn't, read it again, and again, and

The Way It Should Be

AGAIN! When you have time throughout the day, pick up this book. Instead of hanging out or wasting time doing nothing, pick up this book.

Let the messages in this album inspire you to take charge of your destiny. Think about your decisions. Think about the consequences of bad choices. Think about the success of good decisions. Remember to always think about your future. Most importantly, GO GET YOURS!

I leave you with a quote from Minister Benjamin F. Muhammed (Benjamin Chavis). May it inspire you to take charge and control of your destiny.

Brothers help me.

Help me to do what's right.

Help me to stop the slaughter of our children.

Help me put an end to the disrespect and dishonor of our most valuable resource, the black woman.

Help me to put an end to the destruction of the young mind, through the use of drugs and alcohol.

Help me to build up a population of great thinkers. People who create change through thoughtfulness and spirituality.

Will you choose that truth?

Will you?

Will you choose the light over the darkness?

Will you choose light?

It's time.........it's time.........it's time!!!!

Go Get Yours

Minister Benjamin F. Muhammed's speech appears courtesy of the movie *Belly* (1998)

Step Your Game Up

For the record, no man or woman on this earth is perfect. Some damn sure are close to it. The point you should understand is that we all have flaws. We must all strive to do better each and everyday. It's not enough just for you to be a young man. You should aim to be an immaculate young man.

No shame in staying on your GAME

There is nothing soft, weak or lame about a young man who wants to represent himself properly. God made you in a special way and one should always remember that. You should be confident in what you display in the mirror, as well as to the world.

Keepin' it sexy is your life long responsibility. You are responsible for never allowing God's work to become damaged or polluted. Never let the traits or presence that you have depreciate.

Society sometimes gives the impression that you are a homosexual if you are too concerned with your appearance. This way of thinking is by far the most ignorant thought that can enter your brain. Every young man has the right to keep himself on point. This is not gay. Keeping yourself on point simply means that you are staying on top of your game.

Young people who refuse to care about their appearance

only reflect that they do not care about themselves. Those who make an effort, but lack in certain areas simply need to get with the program. They must take strides to improve and restore themselves so that they resemble the strong image that God intended for them to have. If you happen to fall in this category, don't be upset. Do not be discouraged. This just means that it's time for you to step your game up.

Respect Yourself

Keeping yourself groomed should be viewed as a necessity; however, there are many young people who see it as a chore. You can never expect to elevate your game if you're not keeping yourself clean. Walking around with wild hair and bad breath is the look of only a boy. No way can you expect for people to treat you with respect if you disrespect yourself by not practicing good hygiene.

So many members of our young generation fail to realize how potent you can be when you are on your "A" game. When you show yourself to be presentable, people take notice. Your presence commands respect when your game is on point. Choosing not to represent yourself in the right way only leaves a negative impression with those that come in contact with you. Rather than wait to get called out on what you're lacking, take time to see if you need to step up your game.

Ask yourself if you have any of the following:
- grimy finger nails
- bad breath
- wrinkled clothing
- dirty shoes
- foul body odor
- nappy hair

If you have been accused of having any of the above issues, chances are you need to step up your game in the grooming department.

Smell fresh

A foul body odor is an absolute "no no." You cannot expect for a girl to hang around you if you have a funky odor. No young man should have to be told how stinky he smells or that his breath reeks of hot garbage. Take pride in the scent that your body gives off.

The worst habit in the world for a young man is to carry a terrible smell. Bad breath or a sour body odor is considered as only a cry for help. Imagine trying to listen to someone when their breath smells like they rinsed their mouth out with dirty toilet water. The moment they open their mouth you smell only doggie poop.

Do you really want to put your peers through the agony of only smelling what you have to say because your breath smells like fish eggs? Do the world a favor by brushing your teeth and gargling each day with some mouthwash.

Always make an effort to keep yourself smelling good. No person with true potential should be caught walking around smelling foul. A clean scent should be every young man's trademark. Your scent should only enhance your presence, not destroy it. Use quality deodorant, cologne and body spray as necessary so that you smell only like a champion.

Nails

Grimy fingernails have no place on a young man with potential. Someone who is about business keeps his nails clean and short. He doesn't have to worry about contaminating someone's hand when he gives him a firm handshake.

The look of a boy is one with dirty, long fingernails. His nails look as if he's been constantly digging in his nose or in the crack of his ass. Step your game up and stop rocking filthy fingernails. Invest in some fingernail clippers and get with the program.

The same rule applies to toe nails as well. Even if you are an athlete, you can make an effort to keep your feet and nails clean. There's no reason why your feet should look as if you've been walking in the desert or in Ethiopia. Make sure that you are regularly cleaning your feet.

You should not have the room smelling like rotten apples the moment you pull off your sneakers. A man keeps his feet and toenails clean on a daily basis. You don't have to go out and get weekly pedicures, but you can grab a pair of toenail clippers and keep your toenails in check.

Hair

One of the things that are extremely noticeable about today's society is the change in hairstyles. In our lifetime, hairstyles will always change every generation. Years back, guys used to keep a fresh blend or an "even steven." Now it's all about how long can you grow your hair. People can say what they want, but when you get older and interview for a job, what eliminates you from getting a job could be your hairstyle.

When it comes to hair, just understand that in life people are going to look at you and judge you. If you walk around with unkept hair that looks a mess, understand that people may view you as a dirty person. Remember that you only get one chance to make a first impression. Make sure the impression you make on others is one that you can be proud of.

Should you choose to wear your hair short or long, make the effort to keep it clean. Just because you choose to

The Way It Should Be

wear dreadlocks doesn't mean that they have to look a hot mess. You can keep them looking fresh by re-twisting them as needed.

Low cut hair should be shampooed periodically. Facial hair should also be kept clean and trimmed. Don't try to rock a goatee unless you have enough hair on your chin to group a goatee together. Otherwise, keep it low or cut it off until it grows out to how it should look.

Stay fresh

If you choose to carry yourself like a slovenly, sloppy lad, people will see that and treat you accordingly. Dragging when you walk and looking down when you talk shows a lack of confidence. Wearing clothes that do not properly fit your body is a sign of immaturity. Choosing to rock oversized shirts or pants that are too skinny only resemble that you are in need of a mother to come and dress you because you don't know how to.

As far as clothing, make an effort to run an iron over your shirts and pants. You may not be able to afford the high-priced brand names, but that doesn't mean that you have to look like trash. An iron will make even a basic t-shirt and jeans look presentable. Regardless of what you or your parents can afford to buy, there's no excuse for looking run down.

Understand that when you display yourself in public, you become a representation of yourself and your heritage. Be proud of what you represent and make sure that others respect that. Don't be surprised if a person can't honor how you represent yourself if you're dressed like a clown. Make sure that you are clean in your appearance and well groomed.

Body image

This topic may seem uncontainable to our young generation, but some of it can be managed if one chooses to focus on it. Our physical stature goes through many changes as one makes the transition of going from a boy to a young man. Acne, growth spurts, body hair and voice changes all play a pivotal role in this transition. While certain factors are uncontrollable, the one factor that can be controlled is obesity.

Too many of our young people are obese because they are stuffing their face with food and not giving their body enough physical activity. It is unexplainable for a 14-year-old boy to weigh beyond 300 pounds. If this description fits you and you are not pleased, get off your butt and do something about it. Jog around your neighborhood, school track, or at a local park.

Though a diet should not be encouraged for an adolescent, one should be cautious of the types of food that you shove down your throat. If you have an enormous appetite, at least do your best to keep it healthy. Add foods filled with protein and vitamins to your plate, instead of those foods packed with grease and fat. Give carrot sticks a chance sometime before you slam all those Doritos and potato chips down your mouth. Pick up a bottle of water, rather than soft drink after soft drink.

Confidence is the key

No key component in stepping your game up is bigger than CONFIDENCE. The term confidence is probably the most used term in this book. The reason for this is because confidence is required in order for us to achieve the best results possible. People should be able to hear, taste, see and smell confidence whenever you enter into a room. Confidence ought to be demonstrated in your talk and walk.

The way we step our game up does not only apply to our physical appearance or hygiene. We also have to take the time to step our game up mentally. We must begin to challenge ourselves in terms of how we think.

A person with game should possess a mentality that reflects it. Their attitude and body language should be a symbol of poise. Your walk should be nothing less than an example of self-assurance.

The words that you speak should be expressed with affirmation and clarity. No one has to tell confident people to speak up or repeat themselves. When you're sure of yourself, your speech and tone should be a pure reflection. Members of the young generation should make the effort to develop this characteristic each and every day. There's nothing sadder than someone who mumbles and stumbles. Step your game up so that you don't or no longer fall in that trap.

We should view confidence the same way that we view "gravity." In our science classes, we were taught that gravity allows us to stand level while on any surface. We are so use to doing what we consider as normal activities without ever thinking that gravity allows us to walk, stand and sit without falling on our face. Confidence should be considered in the same way.

You should never underestimate yourself in any situation because your confidence allows you to achieve anything. Gravity was always here on earth. We just never knew until some scientist in a lab coat discovered it. Confidence was always stored inside of you. It's up to you to make sure that you discover it. Putting your confidence to use is the biggest key to stepping your game up.

Along with confidence, stepping your game up literally means fine-tuning what you were already born with. God made you the way you are for a special reason. The purpose of this chapter is to encourage you to continue the maintenance on the vehicle that God designed. Carry yourself with the dignity and respect that God intended for you to have.

Again, stepping up your game does not mean completely changing the person that you are. This is what we consider as "fake." Stepping your game up simply means to make adjustments in those areas that require improvement. No one person on this earth is perfect. No one person on this earth will ever be perfect. Yet, we can always seek to get as close to perfection as possible.

For example, Michael Jordan is considered to be the GOAT of basketball. People all over the world dub him as the greatest basketball player of all-time. As great as Michael Jordan was in his career, even he saw parts of his game that could be improved. Jordan never relaxed until he believed without a doubt that he was at his absolute best. He never became complacent with his game. Now if the greatest player that ever lived could see flaws, don't you think that there may be a few things that you can brush up on?

The decision to step up your game is one that only you can make. Be encouraged to improve wherever you have flaws because you want to be the best person you can possibly be. Do it because being at your best is important to you. Whatever reasons you might have, use it as motivation and step your game up.

The Way It Should Be

(Step your game up)

What are some things that you know you can improve upon?

What are some good habits that you can add to your daily or weekly routine?

What are some habits that are preventing you from appearing or being at your best?

Rewind: Take Notes

Excuses

Excuses will never help you move forward, but only backwards.

Excuses only excuse you from achieving progress.

Learn to counter an excuse with a solution.

The people who succeed in this world are those who refuse to make excuses.

Believe

Always believe in yourself and your dreams. Remember that you were born for a purpose. That purpose was to achieve excellence.

Never allow someone else to crush the goals you have set for yourself.

Don't expect for success to come without struggle.
No one should believe in you more than yourself.

Fools

You can't achieve greatness if you spend all your time hanging out with losers. Don't allow yourself to waste time.

Let fools "do what they do," just remember that if you want to succeed you must "do you."

Focus

Staying focused is one of the biggest obstacles in our road to success. We usually let others distract us such as friends, haters, and family. Remember that no one in the industry got where they are today from letting others distract them. If you want to make it to the top, you have to keep your eyes on the prize.

Parents

Your parents only tell you to do what's right because they've been through what you're going through. They want to help you avoid the problems that they've already dealt with in life.

Plan

In life there are so many roads that will come along your way. Don't allow yourself to get confused. Make a plan so that you'll know the right directions to follow.

Rise above the Haters

You may be able to murder a hater, but you can't murder hate. Arm yourself with knowledge, education, and enlightenment. That's the best way to deal with a hater.

Education

Having an education can never hurt, but only help you.

Athletes and entertainers should be the first to seek an education.

Have an interest in learning how to manage your own money.

Never expect for others to look out for your best interest unless you take the initiative to get educated.

Outro

No matter what you have been through during your time on this earth, you can accomplish whatever you put your mind to. Brilliant people are considered brilliant only because they put their mind and efforts toward excelling in beneficial activities. Criminals are considered criminals because they chose to put their mind and efforts toward excelling in destructive or illegal activities. All you have to do is put your energy into doing what will lead you to a productive future.

Excuses are nothing more than reasons that fail to justify why we cannot live up to our potential. Any person that has reached success in this world did not sit back and let what we would consider an excuse stop them from achieving. That person made it a mission to succeed, no matter who or what stood in the way. Every member of the young generation must be encouraged to do the same. Those who oppose can either get down or lay down.

In life, we are treated based on how we represent ourselves. If you act like a youngin,' people will never stop treating you like one. If you want to be respected, you should carry yourself in a way that your behavior will reflect it. The Bible has a scripture that reads, "when I was a child I spoke as a child, but when I became a man I put away childish things." It's up to you to decide when it's time for you to put away those childish things.

Always do what you say you will do. Too many of us talk

about it, but we never do anything. Remember to back up your words with actions. If you say you're going to complete something, honor your word by finishing it. If you say you're going to do something, be about your business and get it done. Your word is your bond. People will never respect it until you begin to stand behind it.

Never expect to receive anything in this world for free. Be expected to work for the things that you want out of life. Be prepared to *grind* for the things that you desire. Your work ethic will eventually provide you with those things you believe you deserve.

Never expect for everything to be fair in your life. God placed each one of us in our own skin and put each of us in unique situations. Your circumstances will always be different from others. Do not view your situation as a disadvantage, but rather see it as motivation to work harder. Do what it takes to ensure that your conditions or surroundings cannot prevent you from succeeding.

Remember to think before you speak during your time on this earth. Refrain from speaking negatively of another if that person has no control or position in your life. Speak words that will lift you up and those around you. Speak phrases that can spark a positive reaction in your peers. You have the ability to control certain things that happen around you.

Never waste time on people who do not have your best interest in mind. Anyone that is seeking to bring you down should not even be worth a minute of your time. Certain people just cannot be killed with kindness. Those people should not deserve your attention.

Time is the most precious asset on this earth. It is the one thing that we can never gain or take back. You can only lose time. The moment you are brought into this world the clock starts ticking. Be careful how you use your time and whom you choose to spend it with.

Try not to dwell on disappointments from the past. Apply your thoughts only on the present and future. Never worry about the past because the past cannot be changed. You must only concentrate on making the most of each day in order to better your future. Don't waste your time on time that you cannot get back!

Remember to appreciate the people who are always there for you. Take time to thank them once in a while. Everybody has at least one person who will always stand in his or her corner. Be grateful for those people that have faith in you and care enough to help you along the way in your quest for excellence.

At some point in our life we are all going to have to work for the things that we want. Even criminals have to work to get what they want. Anyone who is able to live a plentiful lifestyle without ever having to put in a hard day's work is considered to be in the less than 1% of people who are that fortunate. So make it easier on yourself and get acquainted with the idea that you will have to work at some time in your life.

Always make an effort to take advantage of opportunity. Never pass up the chance to gain more for yourself. The world can be difficult enough when we can't see opportunity. Dedicate yourself to seizing the moment when you have a chance to get ahead in your life. So many doors are wide open to us that we never even think to walk through. Lace up your running shoes and start sprinting through those doors.

About the Author

Ivan James was raised in the diverse area of Pensacola, FL. As a talented basketball player in the city of Pensacola, Ivan focused on becoming the best at an early age. He was recognized as a talented athlete and scholar in the classroom. While Ivan made progress in his activities, so many of his promising peers began to scatter along the way.

> *"At a young age, I noticed so many of my friends that had the ability to do great things. I played with kids who had the potential to go*

> *to the NBA and NFL. I sat next to kids who had the brains to become engineers, lawyers or any profession that they chose. The biggest element missing in their lives was discipline. I have no doubt that a lot of people I knew along the way could be in much better positions today. Discipline would have prevented so many from slipping into activities that would harm their future."*

Realizing his potential in academics and entertainment, Ivan continued to work hard. His efforts awarded him the chance to receive an education at Florida A&M University. It was in college that he discovered how many doors are open when you work hard and focus. The opportunity to go to college provided Ivan with higher learning, as well as a network of driven individuals seeking to be successful in the world.

> *"One of the biggest benefits of going to college is having the chance to see other young people with a passion to succeed. A person might be born with the determination for excellence, but college is one of the best places for you to nurture that determination. College provides you with the opportunity to build relationships that can benefit you then, as well as along the way."*

Before receiving his degree in Business Administration in 2006, Ivan created the EMG Foundation. The birth of the foundation sparked even more of a desire for the young man to think of ways to aid his peers on their path to excellence. The idea behind the foundation was to provide financial assistance to students who receive non-paid internships in the entertainment industry.

With such a passion and dedication to help others achieve their potential, it was only a matter of time before he decided to publish a book. *Go Get Yours* is a combination of experiences and messages received by James and re-delivered to the youth of today and tomorrow. Below, James explains his need to write the book, *Go Get Yours*.

> *People have asked me all the time, why write a book? My response is always the same; I have something to say. When I was younger I thought about being a rapper until I realized one thing, I don't rap. By writing a book, I'm able to deliver messages that I would have wanted to say in my music. Writing this book allowed me to address concerns and issues that can't be addressed in music. I saw this book as an opportunity to inform and inspire young people to accomplish their goals.*

In his own words, Ivan managed to observe his surroundings and noticed bad choices that many of his peers made along the way. Rather than continue to pursue a hobby, sport or schoolwork, his peers began to go in the wrong directions. Several friends never reached their potential or utilized their God given talents. After years of watching so many peers fall short of success, Ivan chose to take a stand and help others realize how bright their future can be.

The attempt to better our young people is one that Ivan James feels will never be fulfilled. Until we find a way to control the issues affecting the progress of young people, James believes that each young person will always find an excuse. These issues such as poverty, single-parent households, drug abuse, fatherless homes, teen pregnancy and more must become controlled. So many of these problems can be resolved if we choose to start a new trend, which is to think before we go forth with our actions.

Ivan developed and released Go Get Yours as a way to encourage today's generation to make choices that will only improve their future, not tarnish it. Previous generations may have left our young people to face problems today that were once created in the past. Rather than pass today's problems to future generations, we can make the step to end the cycle. This book is not the answer, but it can spark the ideas and thoughts that can lead to answers.

> *"If we want to achieve our best, we must properly prepare ourselves. There is no blueprint that gives people a perfect route to become successful. Yet, I believe that this book provides the foundation for a person to build upon. If that person sticks with the foundation, he or she will also continue to make the steps that will lead to becoming successful."*

Go Get Yours is the first book published by Mr. James. His work is filled with inspiring messages and a positive humor that helps us to reflect on ourselves. We can be sure to expect for Mr. James to publish more resources dedicated to young people. Ivan continues to put his efforts into projects that will ultimately benefit those seeking to reach their potential. Regardless of how high he may climb up, James is determined to leave a hand to pull others up.

> *"I still consider myself to be a young man. The sky remains as the only limit to how far one can go in this world. No matter what level I may reach, no platform is too large or small to*

connect with those who may need that extra push. Anyone who has made it can and should always give time to extend support to anyone else hoping to make it."

GOD'S WORD
for My Day

READ • TRUST • BELIEVE

God's Word for My Day – Fall Edition
Read. Trust. Believe.

Copyright © 2024 Life Outreach International

All rights reserved. No part of this book may be reproduced or transmitted in any form or by any means, electronic or mechanical, including photocopying, recording, or by any information storage and retrieval system, without permission in writing from the publisher.

Unless otherwise noted, scripture quotations marked NIV are taken from the Holy Bible, New International Version®, NIV®. Copyright © 1973, 1978, 1984, 2011 by Biblica, Inc.™ Used by permission of Zondervan. All rights reserved worldwide. www.zondervan.com The "NIV" and "New International Version" are trademarks registered in the United States Patent and Trademark Office by Biblica, Inc.™

Scripture quotations marked NKJV are taken from the NewKing James Version®. Copyright © 1982 Used by permission. All rights reserved.

ISBN: 978-1-963492-10-1

Assembled and Produced for Life Outreach International by
Breakfast for Seven
breakfastforseven.com

Printed in the United States of America.

Introduction

God's Word for My Day is a unique devotional featuring a daily Scripture, a quick inspirational thought and a designated space for you to journal your thoughts and prayers as you hear God's voice each day.

Divided into four editions – winter, spring, summer and fall – this devotional will encourage you in your faith and help you grow in your relationship with the Lord as you read through the Bible. By journaling your thoughts and listening for God's voice, you are activating, trusting and believing His Word!

READ

TRUST

BELIEVE

September 1

> *He has made everything beautiful in its time. He has also set eternity in the human heart; yet no one can fathom what God has done from beginning to end.*
> (Ecclesiastes 3:11)

When you feel a spiritual longing in your soul, it is because God has set eternity in our hearts! We are aware of life after death because of Jesus. We know that He has conquered death and that through our salvation we are promised an eternity. What a blessing it is to have eternity in your heart and know that something more wonderful than you can imagine awaits you!

Lord, I believe . . .

GOD'S WORD FOR MY DAY — FALL EDITION

September 2

> *Beloved brothers and sisters, we want you to be quite certain about the truth concerning those who have passed away, so that you won't be overwhelmed with grief like many others who have no hope.*
>
> (1 Thessalonians 4:13 TPT)

Paul challenges the Thessalonians, saying they don't have to be *overwhelmed with grief* like unbelievers. We have a new hope, a living hope, a promise that one day we will rise up and meet with Jesus face-to-face alongside every believer who has gone before us. Our hearts may break when we lose a loved one, but we are never without hope. Rest in this promise today.

Lord, I believe . . .

_____
_____
_____
_____
_____
_____
_____
_____
_____
_____
_____

September 3

He makes me lie down in green pastures, he leads me beside quiet waters, he refreshes my soul.

(Psalm 23:2-3)

The Lord is your Shepherd! Feel the refreshing of your soul as you fix your eyes on Jesus today. Imagine walking with Him by still and quiet waters, surrounded by green pastures. You are fulfilled in every way because of our God who provides for you. Remember this peaceful picture today; remind yourself that you are not alone. The Lord is leading you today and every day that follows.

Lord, I believe . . .

September 4

> *For perpetuity God's ways will be passed down from one generation to the next, even to those not yet born. In this way, every generation will set its hope in God and not forget his wonderful works but keep his commandments.* (Psalm 78:6-7 TPT)

Telling the next generation what God has done in your life is how we keep the power of a living faith moving from one generation to the next. Talk about the mighty miracles God has done – miracles from the Bible and miracles from your own life, too. When you begin to talk about all that God has done, it builds your faith and the faith of those around you to believe for more miracles. When you tell your kids, grandkids and even great-grandkids about how the Lord has been faithful in your life, it will stir in them a desire to know God for themselves. Don't wait – start today.

Lord, I believe . . .

September 5

> *My commission is to preach the good news. Yet it is not entirely new, but the fulfillment of the hope promised to us through his prophets in the sacred Scriptures.* (Romans 1:2 TPT)

Did you know Jesus is in every book of the Bible? There are people who think the Old Testament is no longer relevant, but Jesus Himself said He did not come to abolish the law but to fulfill it (Matthew 5:17). Jesus is the fulfillment of all the promises found in the Old Testament! Don't skip the first thirty-nine books of the Bible. The Old Testament is rich with stories of who God is and what He has done for us!

Lord, I believe . . .

September 6

> *"But what is sown on good soil represents those who open their hearts to receive the message and their lives bear good fruit—some yield a harvest of thirty, sixty, even a hundredfold!"* (Mark 4:20 TPT)

The seed is the Word of God. The soil is a person's heart. The simple fact that you are reading this devotional and seeking to gain more understanding of God's Word for your life is a sign you have the seed of the Word of God in the good soil of your heart. For that seed to grow, it's important to spend time in God's presence each day and be a doer of the Word, not just a hearer. If you want to bear abundant fruit, stay close to the vine in sweet relationship with Him.

Lord, I believe . . .

GOD'S WORD FOR MY DAY — FALL EDITION

September 7

> *"You asked, 'Who is this that obscures my plans without knowledge?' Surely I spoke of things I did not understand, things too wonderful for me to know."* (Job 42:3)

Job acknowledges that He has spoken out of turn. How often do we weigh in on matters that we don't fully understand? This comes back to Paul's warning that we be slow to speak. Pray today that God helps you to be more like Job when it comes to admitting your mistakes. God's knowledge is far out of our grasp, and we can't pretend to know all of the wonderful things that He has in store.

Lord, I believe . . .

September 8

> *So we say with confidence, "The Lord is my helper; I will not be afraid. What can mere mortals do to me?"* (Hebrews 13:6)

We are promised that the Lord will never leave us nor forsake us. We are loved by a God who promises unwavering, unfailing love and support for us, so know today that there is nothing to fear. Nothing in this world will ever come close to the power and glory of our Father, so live your life assured of the confidence that comes through putting your faith and hope in Him.

Lord, I believe . . .

September 9

> *. . . and into an inheritance that can never perish, spoil or fade. This inheritance is kept in heaven for you. . . .* (1 Peter 1:4)

Everyone experiences seasons of life that are less than favorable – seasons of rebellion, bitterness, lack of faith. The good news is that we aren't expected to make it through these hard times when we are weak. We know that the Lord is our strength! When our attitudes, words or actions are perishing, spoiling or fading, we know that what is to come will never perish, spoil or fade!

Lord, I believe . . .

September 10

> *"I have not come to call the righteous, but sinners to repentance."* (Luke 5:32)

Jesus never missed an opportunity to witness. His time on earth was spent witnessing at all hours of day and night with people from all different backgrounds. Just as doctors tend to the sick, Christ followers are called to tend to the lost and hurting of this world. We are called to use the opportunities we are given to witness to others and show them the fullness of life that comes through Christ.

Lord, I believe . . .

GOD'S WORD FOR MY DAY — FALL EDITION

"When your faith stands not on the wisdom of man, but the power of God, everything changes."

James Robison

READ

TRUST

BELIEVE

September 11

> *"Have I not commanded you? Be strong and courageous. Do not be afraid; do not be discouraged, for the LORD your God will be with you wherever you go."* (Joshua 1:9)

This special promise should be close to your heart. God is so personal that He has promised to be with you wherever you go. When you have the Lord of Lords, Almighty God, with you for every step you take, there is nothing to fear. You have nothing to be afraid of, nothing to be discouraged about because God is on your side. He is with you today. Pray that you will remember this promise and feel His presence with you.

Lord, I believe . . .

September 12

> *When the people of the city heard the roaring sound, crowds came running to where it was coming from, stunned over what was happening, because each one could hear the disciples speaking in his or her own language.* (Acts 2:6 TPT)

On the day of Pentecost, the Holy Spirit came roaring onto the scene, first like a mighty wind and then with tongues of fire. Each one of the disciples was filled with the Spirit, enabling him or her to speak in many languages, languages they hadn't known before. People came from all around to find out what all the commotion was about, and they were amazed. They were amazed because they could understand what the disciples were saying. When God shows up, miracles appear.

Lord, I believe . . .

September 13

> *Let us not become weary in doing good, for at the proper time we will reap a harvest if we do not give up.* (Galatians 6:9)

Pray for stamina, an energy that is supplied in abundance by the Lord. You may feel worn out today, uninspired by a lack of results. It can be difficult to stay focused and determined in doing good when you don't feel like you are seeing success. Remain patient and faithful in the Lord, and at the proper time, you will reap a bountiful harvest! Be encouraged by this Word today.

Lord, I believe . . .

September 14

> *My fellow believers, when it seems as though you are facing nothing but difficulties, see it as an invaluable opportunity to experience the greatest joy that you can!* (James 1:2 TPT)

Joy is not dependent on your circumstances! Joy is an attitude, and attitudes are a choice. When you have joy deep down in your spirit, you can fight every battle with a positive outlook. James says that trials are an *invaluable opportunity* to experience joy because you can learn and grow from them. *For you know that when your faith is tested it stirs up the power of endurance* (v. 3). Are you going through a trial? Trust God to strengthen you and give you joy, even in the midst of the storm.

Lord, I believe . . .

September 15

> *Lord, what is it about us that you would even notice us? Why do you even bother with us? For man is nothing but a faint whisper, a mere breath. We spend our days like nothing more than a passing shadow.* (Psalm 144:3-4 TPT)

Life is short. David describes the human lifespan as *nothing more than a passing shadow, a faint whisper, a mere breath* in the eyes of God. Isn't it marvelous that God spends so much time and energy drawing us into His embrace, when our lives are fleeting? He is so good to us. But it is precisely because life is short that we should be intentional with our time in getting to know God and being about His business. What is something you can do today to make a difference in someone's life and shine God's light in the world?

Lord, I believe . . .

_____
_____
_____
_____
_____
_____
_____
_____
_____
_____

GOD'S WORD FOR MY DAY — FALL EDITION

September 16

> *For truth is a bright beam of light shining into every area of your life, instructing and correcting you to discover the ways to godly living.*
> (Proverbs 6:23 TPT)

In this passage of Scripture, Solomon describes seven things that *God truly hates* (v. 16): putting others down, spreading lies and rumors, murder, evil in your heart, bragging about your sins, lying under oath and encouraging conflict between friends. When we allow God's truth to shine brightly in our lives, allowing it access to every crevice of our minds and hearts, it leaves no room for any evil thing to grow or fester. Take a moment to invite God to shine His truth over your life today. Is there any forgiveness you've been withholding, or any evidence of sin that has lingered? Allow God to reveal it, so you can be free from it once and for all.

Lord, I believe . . .

September 17

Then Jesus declared, "I am the bread of life. Whoever comes to me will never go hungry, and whoever believes in me will never be thirsty."
(John 6:35)

The Lord is your Shepherd; you shall not want. God promises to be our sustenance. He will provide for your every need – your physical hunger and thirst, but also your spiritual hunger and thirst. You may be looking for something more in your life today, but fix your eyes on Jesus and see that He is all you need.

Lord, I believe . . .

GOD'S WORD FOR MY DAY — FALL EDITION

September 18

> **YAHWEH said to my Lord, the Messiah: "Sit with me as enthroned ruler while I subdue your every enemy. They will bow low before you as I make them a footstool for your feet."** (Psalm 110:1 TPT)

Sitting down and staying put can feel very passive and inactive. But in this verse, it actually means that when you sit down with God, you're choosing to not rely on your own strength and trust that He will defeat every one of your enemies for you. God will fight your battles and bring about your breakthrough. The first and main thing you do is follow His command and sit at His feet, putting your complete trust in Him.

Lord, I believe . . .

September 19

> *"Salt is excellent for seasoning. But if salt becomes tasteless, how can its flavor ever be restored? Your lives, like salt, are to season and preserve. So don't lose your flavor, and preserve the peace in your union with one another."* (Mark 9:50 TPT)

Salt preserves, adds flavor and tenderizes. Jesus wants our lives to be like salt to others. He wants us to *preserve the peace*, strengthen those around us and help soften the hardness in others. A little kindness can go a long way. Taking the time to talk things through, trying to see a situation from the other person's perspective or giving the benefit of the doubt can be forms of adding "salt" to your relationships. We should always seek to leave the lasting flavor of Christ's love and grace in every relationship and encounter.

Lord, I believe . . .

September 20

> *"I will give you a new heart and put a new spirit in you; I will remove from you your heart of stone and give you a heart of flesh."* (Ezekiel 36:26)

When you are saved in Christ, Scripture says you are given a new heart and a new spirit. You may not feel that you have the power to change certain tendencies or habits, but God does! He has an all-transforming power that creates a new life and new identity in Christ. Are you living your life as someone who has been born again?

Lord, I believe . . .

GOD'S WORD FOR MY DAY — FALL EDITION

> *"Even when everything around us shifts and changes, the peace of God is consistent.'"*
>
> Tammy Trent

READ

TRUST

BELIEVE

September 21

> *. . . and to make it your ambition to lead a quiet life: You should mind your own business and work with your hands, just as we told you, so that your daily life may win the respect of outsiders and so that you will not be dependent on anybody.*
>
> (1 Thessalonians 4:11-12)

God provides strength, motivation and energy when we set ourselves to accomplishing tasks. Paul encourages the Church to work with their hands. As humans we are goal-oriented; we strive to work toward an end and feel accomplished when we finish. People respect a person who can set goals and reach them. It doesn't have to be physical labor that you're working at, but set your mind to accomplish a task today, no matter how small, and feel a boost in your attitude!

Lord, I believe . . .

September 22

> *We can all draw close to him with the veil removed from our faces. And with no veil we all become like mirrors who brightly reflect the glory of the Lord Jesus. We are being transfigured into his very image as we move from one brighter level of glory to another. And this glorious transfiguration comes from the Lord, who is the Spirit.*
>
> (2 Corinthians 3:18 TPT)

After Moses encountered God on Mount Sinai, he had to cover his face before the people because they could not handle the sight of God's glory reflected in him. In fact, the people begged Moses to keep his face covered. An encounter with Christ changes everything. When we encounter Christ, the veil is lifted, hearts are opened and we become a reflection of the glory of God. Look for God's reflection in others as you go about your day today!

Lord, I believe . . .

___
___
___
___
___
___
___
___

September 23

> *"God is not human, that he should lie, not a human being, that he should change his mind. Does he speak and then not act? Does he promise and not fulfill?"*
>
> (Numbers 23:19)

We serve an unfailing, unchanging God. While we are fickle, change our minds and fail to follow through on our words, God's promises are always fulfilled. What a blessing it is to have complete trust in our Father whose love for us is constant.

Lord, I believe . . .

September 24

> *The Sovereign LORD is my strength; he makes my feet like the feet of a deer, he enables me to tread on the heights.* (Habakkuk 3:19)

Know today that you are enabled to climb. When you've got hooves like deer, it is a waste of time to sit idle. God's work can come through provision; we are provided the ability to climb high and achieve great things for His Kingdom. Take full advantage of all you are equipped with!

Lord, I believe . . .

September 25

> *Then Jesus said to them, "Why are you fearful? Have you lost your faith in me?" Shocked, they said with amazement to one another, "Who is this man who has authority over winds and waves that they obey him?"* (Luke 8:25 TPT)

It is one thing to be called someone with little faith or to be asked what you're so afraid of, but when Jesus asks, *"Have you lost your faith in me?"* it hits at gut level. When we give in to fear or feed our doubts, when our faith falters, it is our faith in Jesus that has taken the hit. The next time you feel fear rising up, ask yourself, *Have I lost my faith in Him?* If you have, repent, then spend time in prayer and in the Word, because *faith comes by hearing, and hearing by the word of God* (Romans 10:17 NKJV).

Lord, I believe . . .

September 26

> *Trust in the Lord completely, and do not rely on your own opinions. With all your heart rely on him to guide you, and he will lead you in every decision you make.* (Proverbs 3:5 TPT)

God wants to be part of every decision you make. Don't wait until you are in real trouble to ask God for help. He knows the best course of action in all things. When we try to figure things out on our own before going to God, we can create even bigger messes. By trying to do things our way, we are basically saying we know better than God or, at the very least, as much as Him. God sees the full picture. We only see the small sliver in front of us. Take a moment today to relinquish your pride and submit your heart to God and His wisdom for whatever it is you're walking through.

Lord, I believe . . .

September 27

> *I pray that the eyes of your heart may be enlightened in order that you may know the hope to which he has called you, the riches of his glorious inheritance in his holy people. . . .* (Ephesians 1:18)

When our hearts are opened and enlightened, our Spirits are empowered! We readily receive the wisdom and knowledge of the hope we have in our future, and we live faithfully with a supernatural ease! When our hearts are hardened to the promises God has laid out for us, living faithfully is a difficult task. Pray that God enlightens your heart today so that faith comes easily.

Lord, I believe . . .

September 28

> *But you are God's chosen treasure—priests who are kings, a spiritual "nation" set apart as God's devoted ones. He called you out of darkness to experience his marvelous light, and now he claims you as his very own. He did this so that you would broadcast his glorious wonders throughout the world.* (1 Peter 2:9 TPT)

Do you have a safe place where you keep your most treasured valuables? Maybe it is a literal safe or a safe deposit box at a bank. Maybe it is a hope chest, your sock drawer or under your bed. Imagine the safest place in all the world, protected by armed guards, where the most special treasure is held in a place of honor. That chosen treasure is you! You are worth more than precious stones – you are a living stone! You are *priceless in God's sight* (v. 4). He adores you. Be drenched in His mercy and grace!

Lord, I believe . . .

September 29

> *"Then neither do I condemn you," Jesus declared. "Go now and leave your life of sin."* (John 8:11)

Nothing will ever separate you from the love of God. You are promised His companionship for all the days of your life. While we are called to leave lives of sin, we live in a sinful and broken world. Know that you are not condemned today for any of the sin in your life; you are loved! Choose to walk in the Father's grace today, not condemnation.

Lord, I believe . . .

September 30

> *We are hard pressed on every side, but not crushed; perplexed, but not in despair; persecuted, but not abandoned; struck down, but not destroyed.*
> (2 Corinthians 4:8-9)

Defeat is not an option. No matter what adversities you face, place your hope in the Lord today and see that because of His love and strength, you are empowered to push through every difficult situation. You are not crushed or in despair – God is for you. You are not abandoned – He is with you. You are not destroyed – God is your Protector. Trust that He is bigger than whatever you are facing.

Lord, I believe . . .

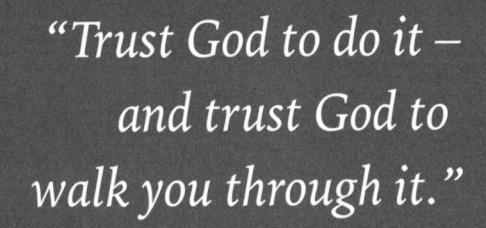

> *"Trust God to do it —
> and trust God to
> walk you through it."*
>
> Randy Robison

READ

TRUST

BELIEVE

October 1

For we know, brothers and sisters loved by God, that he has chosen you. . . . (1 Thessalonians 1:4)

You are a beloved child of God! Paul says here that God chose you – to be loved is to be chosen. As His loved and chosen child, you are entrusted with His Word, and He has faith in you that you will share His Word and be a good example in His name. No matter what we experience from other people, we can always find reassurance in our Father who loves us and has chosen us.

Lord, I believe . . .

October 2

> *. . . because of the truth, which lives in us and will be with us forever. . . .* (2 John 2)

Our salvation through Jesus Christ brings new meaning to truth in our lives. It is the truth of Him that lives in us and stays with us for the entirety of our lives that shapes how we live. When you walk in the truth and hold onto the truth that is within you, God delights in your actions. We may forget that the truth is within us, but it never leaves.

Lord, I believe . . .

GOD'S WORD FOR MY DAY — FALL EDITION

October 3

Recognize the value of every person and continually show love to every believer. Live your lives with great reverence and in holy awe of God. Honor your rulers. (1 Peter 2:17 TPT)

Every person is created by God and has value. The majority of Christian teachings encourage us to value those we consider less fortunate – the poor, the widow, the orphan – and to give to those in need. But do we also *recognize the value of every* political leader, government employee, boss and higher up? This verse reminds us to respect those in authority: *honor your rulers,* and defer to the authority of every human institution, because this is how we show honor and reverence to the Lord.

Lord, I believe . . .

October 4

> *. . . if we are faithless, he remains faithful, for he cannot disown himself.* (2 Timothy 2:13)

Our God is eternally faithful even when we fall short. It's all about Him and never about us. Remember that we are called to love God and one another, and remember to let the light and love of Christ shine through you today.

Lord, I believe . . .

October 5

Therefore confess your sins to each other and pray for each other so that you may be healed. The prayer of a righteous person is powerful and effective. (James 5:16)

What kinds of people have you surrounded yourself with? Community is important to the Christian life as made abundantly clear in the fellowship Jesus shared with His disciples and the early churches that formed as a result. Accountability is important within these communities. Know today that there is strength within the body of Christ – surround yourself with supportive Christians and hold one another accountable.

Lord, I believe . . .

October 6

> *Paul and Silas, undaunted, prayed in the middle of the night and sang songs of praise to God, while all the other prisoners listened to their worship.*
> (Acts 16:25 TPT)

Undaunted means that Paul and Silas weren't discouraged by their imprisonment. They remained resolute despite the painfully difficult situation they had been put into by upsetting the townspeople with their ministry of casting out demons and preaching the Gospel. How could they be so impervious to prison and beatings? Because their hope remained in the Lord. As the psalmist wrote, *for no matter what, I will still sing with praise* (Psalm 42:5 TPT), regardless of circumstances, because He is worthy to be praised! As a result of their praise and worship, their jailer and his entire family came to faith in God. Focus on your source of hope and you will realize that no situation is hopeless!

Lord, I believe . . .

October 7

> *For just one day of intimacy with you is like a thousand days of joy rolled into one! I'd rather stand at the threshold in front of the Gate Beautiful, ready to go in and worship my God, than to live my life without you in the most beautiful palace of the wicked.* (Psalm 84:10 TPT)

Nothing compares to the presence of God. One day with God is better than a thousand with anyone else. You cannot contain a thousand days of joy all rolled into one, nor can you contain the euphoria that *fills those who forever trust in you [Him]* (v. 12). The more you spend time with Him, the more this will become a realization in your life. This yearning and desire to be in God's presence comes when we encounter heaven; and you can encounter heaven on earth right now.

Lord, I believe . . .

October 8

> *"I am the LORD your God, who brought you out of Egypt so that you would no longer be slaves to the Egyptians; I broke the bars of your yoke and enabled you to walk with heads held high."*
>
> (Leviticus 26:13)

Just as God brought the Israelites out of slavery and walked with them through the desert as He led them to the Promised Land, God is working in your life today! He has brought you out of sin and separation from Him. He walks with you today and every day and enables you to walk with your head held high! He gives you power and authority through His Spirit to accomplish great things.

Lord, I believe . . .

October 9

> *Jesus did not let him, but said, "Go home to your own people and tell them how much the Lord has done for you, and how he has had mercy on you."*
> (Mark 5:19)

We are to share the Good News with people around us. We are to show and tell others how much the Lord has done, and we are to extend the mercy that we have received. This is not only for the benefit of others; we benefit ourselves when we recall all of the blessings God has poured out in our lives. When we declare with our mouths that the Lord is good, it gets reinforced in our hearts!

Lord, I believe . . .

October 10

> *"They do not say to themselves, 'Let us fear the LORD our God, who gives autumn and spring rains in season, who assures us of the regular weeks of harvest.'"* (Jeremiah 5:24)

We forget to remember the wonder of creation. Take time to notice and appreciate the changing colors of the leaves or the rain that falls to make the flowers bloom. We take the cycles of nature for granted because God has set everything in perfect working order. Jesus, open our eyes to the beauty and wonder that exists in the creation around us today.

Lord, I believe . . .

_____
_____
_____
_____
_____
_____
_____
_____
_____
_____
_____
_____
_____

GOD'S WORD FOR MY DAY — FALL EDITION

"You will see God's power when you step out in obedience."

Betty Robison

READ

TRUST

BELIEVE

October 11

> *Love makes it impossible to harm another, so love fulfills all that the law requires.* (Romans 13:10 TPT)

Love is the fulfillment of the law. If you look at the Ten Commandments, they are each meant to protect you from doing harm to one another. Murder, stealing, coveting and adultery are all selfish acts that harm others. But Paul says that if we truly love the way God commands us to love, then it is *impossible to harm another*. If you find yourself doing harm to another person – thinking unkind thoughts, saying unkind words, committing a crime against another – then you are not walking in love as God requires of you. Repent of your sins and ask your Heavenly Father to impart His love, love that does no harm to others (or yourself).

Lord, I believe . . .

October 12

> *Be quick to abstain from senseless traditions and legends, but instead be engaged in the training of truth that brings righteousness.* (1 Timothy 4:7 TPT)

The world is full of superstitions and traditions that are quick to offer their own wisdom for your problems. Countless books, articles and talks are given every year – many making promises that guarantee riches, success, health or fame. No matter how loud the world may shout, truth belongs to God. Though many voices may rise, you must be careful to gauge all teaching through the Word of God. Do not give in to the ways of the world. Rather, engage in the training of biblical truth that leads to righteousness. Sow into your spirit and not your flesh. Let your attention be given to the reading of the Word, the exhortation of believers and the doctrines of the faith.

Lord, I believe . . .

_____
_____
_____
_____
_____
_____
_____
_____

October 13

> *You find God's favor by deciding to please God even when you endure hardships because of unjust suffering.* (1 Peter 2:19 TPT)

One of the hardest things can be not defending ourselves against the slander that is spoken against us! But this is precisely the example that Christ left for us. He suffered in our place. He was falsely accused. People spoke terrible things about Him. People condemned Him for being who He was. So, we have to also assume that there will be times when God calls us to endure the same kind of suffering for the sake of the Gospel. Let God be your strength when that time comes!

Lord, I believe . . .

October 14

> *"Worthy is the Lamb, who was slain, to receive power and wealth and wisdom and strength and honor and glory and praise!"* (Revelation 5:12)

God ruled like a lion and suffered like a lamb. He is multifaceted – Jesus is our Shepherd, a gentle Protector and Leader. God is our Father, all-powerful and omnipotent. Glory to God, the Alpha and Omega, the Lion and the Lamb.

Lord, I believe . . .

October 15

> *For you created my inmost being; you knit me together in my mother's womb.* (Psalm 139:13)

You never have to feel unloved or inadequate when you have a relationship with God. He knows every piece of you – even the pieces you hide away and keep secret from people – and yet He still loves you immensely. He knit you together in your mother's womb and created you with a purpose. You are known and loved by our Heavenly Father who put you together piece by piece.

Lord, I believe . . .

October 16

> *"Stand up and praise the LORD your God, who is from everlasting to everlasting. Blessed be your glorious name, and may it be exalted above all blessing and praise."* (Nehemiah 9:5)

This call to praise reminds us of the infinite nature of our God. He is *from everlasting to everlasting* – an endless source of wisdom, grace, mercy and love. Exalt Him today and rejoice in the blessings that flow, without ceasing, from our Father's glorious name.

Lord, I believe . . .

October 17

> *"So this is my command: Love each other deeply, as much as I have loved you. For the greatest love of all is a love that sacrifices all. And this great love is demonstrated when a person sacrifices his life for his friends."* (John 15:12-13 TPT)

Jesus loved us enough to sacrifice His life, His all, for us. He tells us to love others as much as He has loved us. That is a powerful charge! The greatest love you could ever have is to lay down your life for another. This is the manner of love that the Father has given us. Our guiding example of what love is and what it means to love someone else was given to us through Jesus. Love others as Jesus has loved you.

Lord, I believe . . .

October 18

> *. . . do not harden your hearts as you did in the rebellion, during the time of testing in the wilderness. . . .* (Hebrews 3:8)

You may be going through a rough patch in your life but pray today that God helps you to open your heart. When we keep our hearts open and yield ourselves to Him, He is able to work in us and through us. He can shape and mold our hearts to look more like Jesus today. Ask for His great healing and pray that He keeps you from a hardened heart.

Lord, I believe . . .

October 19

> *Let every word you speak be drenched with grace and tempered with truth and clarity. For then you will be prepared to give a respectful answer to anyone who asks about your faith.* (Colossians 4:6 TPT)

If we are going to make God known to others, we have to be prepared to answer when we are asked about our faith. In this verse, Paul advises us to keep four things in mind: grace, truth, clarity and respect. Graceful words are compassionate words. Truthful words will make others thirsty to know more of God. Clear words reveal the simplicity of Jesus's message: *For if you publicly declare with your mouth that Jesus is Lord and believe in your heart that God raised him from the dead, you will experience salvation* (Romans 10:9 TPT). Spoken with respect, your clear words of grace and truth will make Him known.

Lord, I believe . . .

October 20

> *"But I tell you, love your enemies and pray for those who persecute you. . . ."* (Matthew 5:44)

Even as He suffered on the cross, Jesus prayed for the men who had persecuted and ultimately crucified Him. The grace of Jesus knows no bounds, and we are called to mirror His great love and compassion for the world. You are sure to have relationships with people that you don't like – people who are mean or frustrating or challenge your beliefs. Be faithful in praying for them.

Lord, I believe . . .

GOD'S WORD FOR MY DAY — FALL EDITION

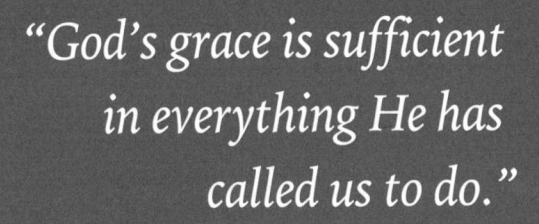

> *"God's grace is sufficient in everything He has called us to do."*

Betty Robison

READ

TRUST

BELIEVE

October 21

> *I can do all this through him who gives me strength.* (Philippians 4:13)

Your strength comes through the Lord when you allow Him to work through you and in you. Your strength to face difficult circumstances, challenges or just another day comes from an all-powerful God. When you feel that you can't do something, look to the Lord who is your strength. Pray to see the strength of the Lord manifest in your life in the areas you feel weakest.

Lord, I believe . . .

October 22

> *"But in spite of this, there is still hope for Israel."*
> (Ezra 10:2)

Even after turning their backs to God and committing sin, the people of Israel realized they had done wrong. They confessed their sin, submitted to the will of God and took responsibility for their actions. Even after big mistakes, there is always hope. Just as there was hope for Israel, there is hope for you! Regardless of your past mistakes, God is ready for you to turn back to Him.

Lord, I believe . . .

October 23

> *For we are God's handiwork, created in Christ Jesus to do good works, which God prepared in advance for us to do.* (Ephesians 2:10)

As God's handiwork, a work of art created by the heavenly hands of the Father, you are equipped to do good works during your time on earth. You don't have to do works to earn your salvation, as it is freely given to us, but good works can be an exciting way to express your gratitude and praise to God while in your earthy body. Good works are an easy way to put our faith in action!

Lord, I believe . . .

October 24

> *In reality, the truth of God is known instinctively, for God has embedded this knowledge inside every human heart.* (Romans 1:19 TPT)

The fingerprints of God are upon you! Knowing right from wrong, truth from fiction, God above all else is instinctual. It is part of our human nature, embedded in us from the moment God imagined our existence. It's like having a beacon – a homing device – inside your heart that draws you to God and to goodness, love and truth. Ignorance is not an excuse for misbehavior, immorality, idolatry or running headlong into darkness. God has given us the freedom to choose but not without consequence. Choose the Truth. Choose the Light. Choose the God who made all things!

Lord, I believe . . .

October 25

> *Here's my point. A stingy sower will reap a meager harvest, but the one who sows from a generous spirit will reap an abundant harvest.* (2 Corinthians 9:6 TPT)

People either give out of a poverty or abundance mindset. People who give with a poverty mindset worry that they do not, or will not, have enough for themselves. They don't trust God to replenish their supply, even if He has in the past. Whereas a person with a mindset of abundance trusts that God will readily supply all that they need. They don't give because it's the law; they give because they have experienced God's extravagant grace. Ironically, each of these types of people are right because God gives little to those who can only be trusted with little, and He gives much to those who can be trusted with more and more.

Lord, I believe . . .

GOD'S WORD FOR MY DAY — FALL EDITION

October 26

> *For in him was created the universe of things, both in the heavenly realm and on the earth, all that is seen and all that is unseen. Every seat of power, realm of government, principality, and authority—it all exists through him and for his purpose! He existed before anything was made, and now everything finds completion in him.*
> (Colossians 1:16-17 TPT)

God is holding you together. You may not feel it, you may not know it, but the same God who holds the universe together by His Word is also holding you. He is not distant, and He is not indifferent toward you. The reminder for you today from Colossians 1 is that you were created by God, you were created for God, and He has a good plan for you. Let anxiety go. Lay hold of the truth that you don't have to hold it all together because God has already promised to do that for you.

Lord, I believe . . .

_____
_____
_____
_____
_____
_____
_____

October 27

> *I have fought an excellent fight. I have finished my full course with all my might and I've kept my heart full of faith.* (2 Timothy 4:7 TPT)

When you near the end of your time on earth, what will be the greatest achievement or summary of your life? What kind of legacy do you want to leave for this world? Death is inevitable, but what we do while we live is up to us. We can fight the good fight, or we can sit on the sidelines. We can finish the course, or we can give up halfway through the race. We can keep the faith, or we can succumb to our doubts. The three Fs of Paul's life are a worthy example of a life well-lived: faith, fight, finish.

Lord, I believe . . .

October 28

> *"Where you die I will die, and there I will be buried. May the LORD deal with me, be it ever so severely, if even death separates you and me."*
> (Ruth 1:17)

This commitment from Ruth is spoken to Naomi, but it is also a commitment to God. Ruth decides to leave everything behind and allow Naomi to lead her into a relationship with God. There is a powerful internal voice that speaks to Ruth and lets her know that, while difficult, this is the best decision for her life. How can you commit to God today?

Lord, I believe . . .

October 29

> *"And who knows but that you have come to your royal position for such a time as this?"* (Esther 4:14)

There are no accidents in God's Kingdom. You are where you are for a specific purpose. Trust in God's timing even when it doesn't match your own. Pray for patience and confidence in our Father's plan for your life. Move in the Spirit and know that you are where you are for a reason.

Lord, I believe . . .

GOD'S WORD FOR MY DAY — FALL EDITION

October 30

> *"And you, little Bethlehem, are not insignificant among the clans of Judah, for out of you will emerge the Shepherd-King of my people Israel!"*
> (Matthew 2:6 TPT)

Have you ever felt insignificant? Overlooked? Unseen? Like God was using everyone around you for a grand purpose except you? Then this verse is for you: *"You, little Bethlehem, are not insignificant!"* Bethlehem was very small in size. David, the youngest and smallest of his brothers, came from tiny Bethlehem. Like David, you have been called! When God does the calling, it is significant. You have a purpose. You are gifted. Every gift from God is a blessing to the recipient and to others. No matter how small your God-given task may seem in the eyes of the world, it is not insignificant to God.

Lord, I believe . . .

GOD'S WORD FOR MY DAY — FALL EDITION

"As we grow in our understanding of God's character, may we also grow in the absolute truth that not one thing in this world can separate us from His love."

Tammy Trent

READ

TRUST

BELIEVE

October 31

> *"A good man brings good things out of the good stored up in his heart, and an evil man brings evil things out of the evil stored up in his heart. For the mouth speaks what the heart is full of."* (Luke 6:45)

Our heart is the wellspring of life. The feelings and thoughts we harbor internally will eventually come out. When we have good things stored in our hearts, our mouths will reflect that by speaking words of love and kindness toward others. However, when we have evil things and negativity in our hearts, our mouths will prove to be ugly reflections of that.

Lord, I believe . . .

November 1

> *A good name is more desirable than great riches; to be esteemed is better than silver or gold.* (Proverbs 22:1)

Having a good name means having a positive reputation, a character of integrity and a spirit that honors and praises God through your actions. Ask yourself whether or not you are showing love toward others through your actions today. We are entrusted with communicating the message of the Gospel, so it is important to portray ourselves as people of true love and integrity.

Lord, I believe . . .

November 2

> *"Your servant has nothing there at all," she said, "except a small jar of olive oil."* (2 Kings 4:2)

Just like in the story of the woman with nothing but a small jar of olive oil, Jesus can do great things through us and sustain us even when we feel like we have nothing to offer. When this woman trusts Elisha for help, her desperation is turned to hope. When we allow God to use what we have, He sustains us. He carries us through times of struggle and reminds us that He is our perfect Provider.

Lord, I believe . . .

November 3

> *And God said, "Let there be light," and there was light. God saw that the light was good, and he separated the light from the darkness.* (Genesis 1:3-4)

Know in your heart today that all *good* things come from our Heavenly Father. He spoke light into existence and from Him all light flows. Our Father couldn't wait even one day to flood the darkness with His light. There's a reason why that was first on His agenda – light changes everything. As we follow in His example, we should spread the light that He gave us with the same sort of urgency and expectation.

Lord, I believe . . .

November 4

> *And since we are his true children, we qualify to share all his treasures, for indeed, we are heirs of God himself. And since we are joined to Christ, we also inherit all that he is and all that he has. We will experience being co-glorified with him provided that we accept his sufferings as our own.*
>
> (Romans 8:17 TPT)

When a person dies and leaves an inheritance, they usually leave it to a person, people or an organization they cared about. As a true child of God, you are a co-heir with Christ in *all his treasures*. He loves you and entrusts everything He has to your care. Live with the knowledge that God has claimed you as His child and declared you co-heir with His Son.

Lord, I believe . . .

GOD'S WORD FOR MY DAY — FALL EDITION

November 5

> *Therefore encourage one another and build each other up, just as in fact you are doing.*
>
> (1 Thessalonians 5:11)

Think about the influence that both positive and negative people have in your life. It can be draining to be around someone who is negative, and often they can bring out negativity in others. However, positive people often bring out positivity in those around them. Make a conscious effort to be more positive and see how it affects those around you.

Lord, I believe . . .

November 6

He said to me: "It is done. I am the Alpha and the Omega, the Beginning and the End. To the thirsty I will give water without cost from the spring of the water of life." (Revelation 21:6)

He is the Alpha and the Omega, the Beginning and the End. Jesus came so that we could have life, and when He returns, it will be to call us to our forever home. Our spiritual thirst is satisfied by His living water, and He continues to sustain our every need. From the beginning to the end, He is with us. Thank Him for the blessing of His living water in your life.

Lord, I believe . . .

November 7

> *For it's not merely knowing the law that makes you right with God, but doing all that the law says that will cause God to pronounce you innocent.*
> (Romans 2:13 TPT)

We all know that running a red light while driving is against the law. But knowing the law isn't enough; you actually have to stop at the red light! If you are caught breaking the law, a judge will find you guilty. Paul is saying the same thing in his letter to the Romans. It's not enough to know the laws – you have to obey the laws if you want to honor God. If you love Him, you will keep His commands! (John 14:15-17). Is there any area in your life where you have disobeyed God? Out of your love for God, choose now to repent and obey, no matter the cost.

Lord, I believe . . .

November 8

> *"For here is the way God loved the world—he gave his only, unique Son as a gift. So now everyone who believes in him will never perish but experience everlasting life."* (John 3:16 TPT)

If you had to summarize the entire Gospel message into one verse, John 3:16 is the verse that most people would choose. It's a verse widely known; but oftentimes, we're so familiar with it that we forget just how powerful it is. God loves you! So much so that He willingly sacrificed His only Son for you, providing a way for you, and all of humanity, to enjoy an everlasting life with Him in heaven. The Passion Translation emphasizes that this is *"a gift"* to all who believe, proof of God's love for people. Take a moment to meditate on the amazing wonder and beautiful hope found in this gift.

Lord, I believe . . .

GOD'S WORD FOR MY DAY — FALL EDITION

November 9

> *"I the LORD do not change. So you, the descendants of Jacob, are not destroyed."* (Malachi 3:6)

In a world of constant change, we serve a God who tells us that He doesn't change. He moves in our lives, constantly at work for our benefit, but He is not a God who changes. He is the Great I Am – a perfect and holy Father, and He will never be anything else. He is an unchanging anchor for us in times of turbulence and uncertainty.

Lord, I believe . . .

GOD'S WORD FOR MY DAY — FALL EDITION

"Jesus is the center of our life. In the face of any storm, He gives us peace."

James Robison

READ

TRUST

BELIEVE

November 10

> *Each of you should use whatever gift you have received to serve others, as faithful stewards of God's grace in its various forms.* (1 Peter 4:10)

Use your gifting as an extension of God's grace and praise Him while doing so. There is purpose behind your talents and special abilities, and we are called to use them as a form of serving others. Ask God to reveal to you what your gifts are so that you may put them to good work in the lives of those around you.

Lord, I believe . . .

November 11

> *"But seek first his kingdom and his righteousness, and all these things will be given to you as well."*
> (Matthew 6:33)

Our first objective every day should be to seek God's Kingdom and His righteousness. After that, our earthly needs like food, clothing and shelter come. When we seek God's Kingdom and come to know His righteousness, we find that He provides all that we truly need. Apply this to other areas of your life – how can you seek His Kingdom and righteousness at work? As a parent? As a friend?

Lord, I believe . . .

November 12

> *Jesus said to him, "What do you mean 'if'? If you are able to believe, all things are possible to the believer." When he heard this, the boy's father cried out with tears, saying, "I do believe, Lord; help my little faith!"* (Mark 9:23-24 TPT)

In this passage, the biggest hurdle the father had to overcome was believing that Jesus could heal his son. He had faith, but he knew it was small. He was honest with Jesus in his request. The healing he so desperately sought was granted to him, and so was the increase of his faith. Everything became possible after belief. Like He did for the father in Mark 9, God will meet you right where you're at. Talk to the Lord and be honest about everything on your heart. And then be ready for God to reveal more of His plans to you as you trust and follow Him!

Lord, I believe . . .

November 13

> *Dear friends, now we are children of God, and what we will be has not yet been made known. But we know that when Christ appears, we shall be like him, for we shall see him as he is.* (1 John 3:2)

The Bible doesn't give us all the answers. We don't know what life after death holds for us — we don't know what heaven will be like. But His Word does tell us that we shall be like Christ when He returns. Because of God's great love for His children, we will become like Christ, the Savior who took our place on the cross, and we will be blessed with an eternal communion with our Father!

Lord, I believe . . .

November 14

> *Therefore, there is now no condemnation for those who are in Christ Jesus, because through Christ Jesus the law of the Spirit who gives life has set you free from the law of sin and death.* (Romans 8:1-2)

Because of Jesus, you are free to live a life covered by His grace. You are not condemned for any past or future actions; you are free through Christ. Today, know that no matter how you may feel about yourself, God does not condemn you. Allow your mind to be Kingdom-focused. This doesn't mean we should sin freely and without worry; it means that when we inevitably fail, the Lord's love will not stop flowing over us.

Lord, I believe . . .

GOD'S WORD FOR MY DAY — FALL EDITION

November 15

> *If I speak in the tongues of men or of angels, but do not have love, I am only a resounding gong or a clanging cymbal.* (1 Corinthians 13:1)

The importance of love, especially when speaking to others, can be the difference between a pleasant melody and a clanging cymbal. We want our words to be heard and understood by others, and to fulfill this desire, we are told that we must have love. Love is given freely by God, and when we have love in our hearts, we can also give it freely through our words and actions.

Lord, I believe . . .

November 16

> *Your hand-to-hand combat is not with human beings, but with the highest principalities and authorities operating in rebellion under the heavenly realms . . . Because of this, you must wear all the armor that God provides so you're protected as you confront the slanderer, for you are destined for all things and will rise victorious.* (Ephesians 6:12-13 TPT)

God has given you everything you need for victory! He has equipped you with a complete set of armor to wear into battle. He has equipped you with truth, righteousness, peace, faith, salvation and the Word of God. The key to victory is knowing who you are up against. You are not at war with people, but with the *highest principalities and authorities operating in rebellion under the heavenly realms*. Stand firm and put on your full battle array that the Lord has provided for you. By faith and the armor of God, victory is yours.

Lord, I believe . . .

November 17

> *Just as it is written: "As surely as I am the Living God, I tell you: 'Every knee will bow before me and every tongue will confess the truth and glorify me!'" Therefore, each one must answer for himself and give a personal account of his own life before God.*
> (Romans 14:11-12 TPT)

The beginning of Romans 14 instructs us to not judge others harshly. We are only accountable for our lives because one day *every knee will bow . . . and every tongue will confess the truth. . . .* So set your heart before God each day, seek to become like Christ, read and obey the Word of God. Take account of your life, actions and fruit. It is wise to choose to live each day wholly for Him. Consider the words of Romans 14: one day we will stand before the living God and give a personal account of our lives before Him, confessing the truth and glorifying Him.

Lord, I believe . . .

GOD'S WORD FOR MY DAY — FALL EDITION

November 18

> *The Lord is not slow in keeping his promise, as some understand slowness. Instead he is patient with you, not wanting anyone to perish, but everyone to come to repentance.* (2 Peter 3:9)

The timing of God and our timing are two very different things. God is patient with you today and every day. When we demand answers, desperate for His promises to come to fruition, He patiently waits for things to fall into place – things that we might be unaware of. Trust in God's timing today and know that the Father is patient with you and is working things for your good.

Lord, I believe . . .

November 19

> *When you discover something sweet, don't overindulge and eat more than you need, for excess in anything can make you sick of even a good thing.*
> (Proverbs 25:16 TPT)

Proverbs tells us there is such a thing as too much of a good thing. In this verse, Solomon is saying a few bites of cheesecake may be delicious but eating the whole cake can make you sick. Practical and profound wisdom for life is found in Proverbs. There is ample supply of advice and insight that is applicable for big decisions and daily living. Proverbs is truly God's gift to us as believers to save us from days of heartache or a lifetime of regret. If you make it a priority to read, study and put into practice the things you learn in Proverbs, you will *reign in life* (Proverbs 1:1 TPT).

Lord, I believe . . .

_____
_____
_____
_____
_____
_____
_____
_____
_____

"When you respond in obedience to the Word of God, the transformation of your life will overflow onto everyone around you."

Tammy Trent

READ

TRUST

BELIEVE

November 20

> *Be devoted to tenderly loving your fellow believers as members of one family. Try to outdo yourselves in respect and honor of one another.*
> (Romans 12:10 TPT)

Do you want to transform your relationships? Read Romans 12! Paul's advice to the Romans can make your relationships feel like heaven on earth. He writes, *Take a constant interest in the needs of God's beloved people and respond by helping them. And eagerly welcome people as guests into your home. Speak blessing . . . Celebrate with those who celebrate, and weep with those who grieve . . . be as mindful of another's worth as you are your own . . . Never hold a grudge. Do your best to live as everybody's friend* (vv. 13-17). In other words, treat everyone like family, make everyone feel at home, take care of one another, and you will overcome evil with good.

Lord, I believe . . .

November 21

> *"Let us acknowledge the LORD; let us press on to acknowledge him. As surely as the sun rises, he will appear; he will come to us like the winter rains, like the spring rains that water the earth."* (Hosea 6:3)

His presence is always with you – press on to acknowledge Him! When you find yourself caught up in stress or busyness during your day, acknowledge God. Take time to pray and talk with Him. As the sun rises and as the rain falls, the Lord will continue to appear in your life day after day. Remind yourself to press on in your relationship with Him, taking time to experience His sweet presence.

Lord, I believe . . .

November 22

> *Be well balanced and always alert, because your enemy, the devil, roams around incessantly, like a roaring lion looking for its prey to devour. Take a decisive stand against him and resist his every attack with strong, vigorous faith. . . .*
> (1 Peter 5:8–9 TPT)

Ask yourself: *Am I living a well-balanced life?* If the answer is yes, you are much more likely to be able to stand against the Devil when he attacks. But if the answer is no, you are setting yourself up to be devoured by his tactics. God wants us to live balanced lives, with our priorities in line with His, saying yes to the things He calls and equips us to do and no to the things that are not ours to carry. Take time today to do a personal assessment. If you feel stretched too thin, ask God where you are out of balance and take the steps needed to strengthen your faith.

Lord, I believe . . .

November 23

> *Dear friend, do not imitate what is evil but what is good. Anyone who does what is good is from God. Anyone who does what is evil has not seen God.*
>
> (3 John 11)

When we get a glimpse of who our Father truly is, Scripture tells us we are deeply changed by the transforming love and power that comes from Him. With Jesus in your heart, you will gravitate toward goodness. Those who do evil do not truly know God and have not experienced His grace and presence in their lives. What a beautiful blessing to commune with our Father!

Lord, I believe . . .

November 24

> *"Here I am! I stand at the door and knock. If anyone hears my voice and opens the door, I will come in and eat with that person, and they with me."*
>
> (Revelation 3:20)

Jesus knocking at the door of the lukewarm Church is a reminder of the importance of being part of a community that is on fire for God. Many churches are lukewarm, and in order for Jesus to enter, they must repent and fully embrace Jesus. Are you part of a community that is on fire for God? Is He knocking at the door of your church or is He already inside?

Lord, I believe . . .

November 25

> *For to us a child is born, to us a son is given, and the government will be on his shoulders. And he will be called Wonderful Counselor, Mighty God, Everlasting Father, Prince of Peace.* (Isaiah 9:6)

The greatest gift the world ever received was the gift of Jesus Christ. God sent His Son – full of wisdom when our understanding fails, full of might when our strength fails, everlasting when we are finite and peaceful despite the sin that covers His creation. Jesus is our Savior, able to meet every need.

Lord, I believe . . .

November 26

> *Be merciful to those who doubt. . . .* (Jude 22)

Jesus calls us to make disciples in His name. You are sure to encounter those who doubt the Gospel if you haven't already, but we are told to be merciful to them. Show love and kindness to anyone who may struggle to find faith. Pray for patience today in witnessing to those around you. Just as you are extended mercy from the Lord, extend mercy to others.

Lord, I believe . . .

November 27

> *For the wages of sin is death, but the gift of God is eternal life in Christ Jesus our Lord.* (Romans 6:23)

Sin is the ultimate separator between you and God. Even when you are saved, sin is to be taken seriously because it can distract you from your relationship with God. Don't allow your eyes to be pulled from the end goal of an eternity with the Father because of earthly temptation or sin.

Lord, I believe . . .

November 28

> *But Hezekiah prayed for them, saying, "May the LORD, who is good, pardon everyone who sets their heart on seeking God—the LORD, the God of their ancestors—even if they are not clean according to the rules of the sanctuary."* (2 Chronicles 30:18-19)

We are imperfect and we will fail. Thank God for His grace and mercy that when we fail, even when we set out with good intentions, He harbors no disappointment or ill will toward us. We are pardoned and washed clean from our sin. God is so good, and He knows and understands that even when we set out to do good, things do not always go as planned.

Lord, I believe . . .

November 29

> *Little children, you can be certain that you belong to God and have conquered them, for the One who is living in you is far greater than the one who is in the world.* (1 John 4:4 TPT)

Nothing and no one is more powerful than God. No temptation is greater than Him. No power of darkness can overcome Him. His love is in you. He created you. You are His seed; the very essence of God is within you, leading and guiding you. You belong to Him. Therefore, you are an overcomer! Be certain today that you belong to God and no power can separate you from His love. Take heart that the One who is living in you is far greater than the one who is in the world.

Lord, I believe . . .

November 30

> *"My old identity has been co-crucified with Christ and no longer lives . . . My new life is empowered by the faith of the Son of God who loves me so much that he gave himself for me, dispensing his life into mine!"* (Galatians 2:20 TPT)

Your identity is who you are. Paul said that his old identity was gone and that he had new life in Christ. Everything that his former self believed in, lived for, identified with was no longer true for him. He had a new life and identity that stemmed from *"the Son of God who loves me so much that he gave himself for me."* The same is true for you. The old has gone, the new has come. Your new life in Christ is empowered by faith in the Son of God. He is the One who loves you and gave Himself for you. Your life is now hidden with Christ forever.

Lord, I believe . . .

GOD'S WORD FOR MY DAY — FALL EDITION